Please Return

When Your Child
Has Been Molested

Kathryn Brohl
with
Joyce Case Potter

When Your Child Has Been Molested

A Parents' Guide to Healing and Recovery

Revised Edition

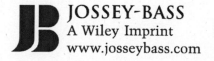
JOSSEY-BASS
A Wiley Imprint
www.josseybass.com

Published by Jossey-Bass
A Wiley Imprint
989 Market Street, San Francisco, CA 94103-1741   www.josseybass.com

Library of Congress Cataloging-in-Publication Data

Brohl, Kathryn.
    When your child has been molested : A parents' guide to healing and
recovery / Kathryn Brohl with Joyce Case Potter.—Rev. ed.
        p. cm.
Includes bibliographical references and index.
    ISBN 978-0-7879-7103-8
    1. Child sexual abuse—United States.   2. Sexually abused
children—United States—Psychology.   3. Child sexual
abuse—Investigation—United States.   4. Sexually abused
children—United States—Family relationships.   5. Sexually abused
children—Counseling of—United States.   I. Potter, Joyce Case, date.
II. Title.
    HV6570.2.B76 2004
    362.76—dc22   2003015270

REVISED EDITION
PB Printing   10 9

Contents

Reality Checks ix

Introduction xi

1. Learning Your Child Has Been Molested 1

2. Reporting Child Sexual Abuse: Investigation and Prosecution Stages 17

3. Supporting Your Child After His Disclosure 27

4. Physical and Emotional Signs of Child and Youth Sexual Abuse 45

5. Your Professional Support Team 59

6. The Formal/Forensic Interview: Helping Investigators Work Effectively with Your Child ... 65

7. The Judicial Process: Why It Takes a While 77

8. Understanding Grief Stages and Secondary Traumatic Stress 87

9. Working with a Counselor 103

10. Helping Your Child Recover 115

11. The Impact on Family Members 129

12. Strengthening Family Communication 135

13. Dealing with Extended Family and Others 145

14. When You or Your Child Must Appear in Court   153

15. When the Sexual Abuse Is Incest   165

16. You Know Your Family Is Getting

     Better When . . .   179

Glossary   189

Additional Information   197

Resources   203

About the Authors   207

Index   209

Reality Checks

Throughout the book, you will find facts about child sexual abuse and other relevant pieces of information in the "Reality Checks" sections.

Reality Check 1: Child Sexual Abuse Definition 3

Reality Check 2: Facts That Challenge Misconceptions About Child Sexual Abuse and Child Molesters 4

Reality Check 3: What to Say to Your Child 30

Reality Check 4: The Progression of Seduction 36

Reality Check 5: What Can Happen If You Don't Support Your Child 40

Reality Check 6: Sexual Development in Children 45

Reality Check 7: Sexual Abuse Signs and Symptoms 53

Reality Check 8: Establishing Reasonable Expectations with Your Child 67

Reality Check 9: Behaviors to Avoid 89

Reality Check 10: Inappropriate Ways to Express Your Anger 90

Reality Check 11: Depression Symptoms 93

Reality Check 12: Acceptance Behaviors
and Attitudes   97

Reality Check 13: Therapist Selection Questions   105

Reality Check 14: Realistic Expectations About
Counseling   112

Reality Check 15: Helping Your Child Feel Safe and
Supporting Her Toward Positive Self-Perception   116

Reality Check 16: Family Communication
Breakdown Signs   135

Reality Check 17: Improving Family
Communication   142

Reality Check 18: What to Keep in Mind When
You're Thinking About Talking to Other People   146

Reality Check 19: What Others May Say   149

Reality Check 20: Preparing Your Child to Appear
in Court   156

Reality Check 21: How You Know When Your
Family Is Better   180

Introduction

The first edition of this book, written in 1988, was one of the few guides available at that time to parents of sexually molested children. Since then, we have learned more about child sexual abuse; we now know about the impact of terrifying experiences (such as sexual assault) on brain function and Secondary Traumatic Stress. This new edition contains this updated material about child and adolescent sexual molestation.

Because of the limited opportunities to learn about the legal and psychological consequences of child sexual assault, which are complex and often long-term, parents can be confounded by their situation. Dealing with the sexual abuse of a child is frequently a confusing and lonely experience.

This book provides information and advice. When caregivers know the facts and apply the interventions suggested here, they are better skilled to work with authorities, cope with personal anxiety, and participate in their child's healing.

This book can be read from beginning to end or by chapter topic. For instance, if a child abuse report has already been made, you may wish to skip to the formal, or forensic, interview section. Or you may want to immediately read about how you can help your child recover, a topic covered in Chapter Ten.

"Reality checks" are provided throughout the text. Compare these with your personal experience, and use them to clarify any preconceived ideas you may have about child and youth sexual assault. These reality markers are reassuring because they let you know that you are not alone.

The Glossary at the end of the book defines terms that are familiar to legal and social work professionals but not to all laypeople. For example, the word *molest* is listed in most dictionaries as a verb, that is, as an action word that means "to accost and harass sexually." Social work professionals also define it as a noun and refer to it as the "molest." If you need further explanation about other terms, don't hesitate to ask one of the professionals you are working with. And you may find it helpful to scan the Glossary before you begin reading the book. You may also wish to look at the Resources and Additional Information as well.

Throughout this book, we have alternated using *he* and *she* by chapter to refer to the child or adolescent victim.

The Thompson family, including Scott, the child victim, whom you will meet throughout this book, is a composite of children and families. Its members are "real" in that they represent families whose lives have been disrupted by child and youth sexual abuse.

The sexual assault described within the story does not indicate any bias on our part against homosexuality. Fondling of boys by older men is only one of many types of sexual molestation. And the concerns that Scott voices reflect normal child development.

If you have already experienced a portion of the investigation or legal process by the time you begin reading this book, don't be discouraged if you realize you've made some mistakes pertaining to the case. It's preferable to correct them, but when that's not possible, forgive yourself for having done your best.

Remember that outside help is necessary when you begin to intervene on behalf of your child. Be sure to seek professional aid that includes counseling, law enforcement, or legal assistance or all three.

We hope this book becomes a friendly reference and provides you with the information and support you need now. You have taken a positive step by seeking out reading material that can guide you through your family's recovery process.

ACKNOWLEDGMENTS

Without our senior editor, Alan Rinzler, this revised edition could not have been written. Alan recognized the need to update the material to make it relevant for our times. Thank you, Alan. And thanks to Seth Schwartz, Jossey-Bass editorial assistant, for handling many details.

A lot has been learned about child sexual abuse since this book was first written. For their contribution in helping to bring it into the twenty-first century, we thank Roger Gunder, Ph.D., Jay Whitworth, M.D., Wayne Cissel, Valerie Stanley, and Saundra Brookshire. Special thanks to friend and colleague Paree Stivers, Ph.D. Her insightful comments contributed greatly to this book. And thanks to attorney Brian Cook for his valuable legal advice.

Finally, we extend our sincere thanks to the original contributors who were pathfinders in working with sexually abused children.

We also wish to acknowledge the family therapists and sexual abuse counselors who suggested developing this updated edition after years of recommending and sharing the first edition with clients. We very much appreciate their gracious comments concerning the contribution that the original edition has made to the healing process.

Kathryn Brohl
Joyce Case Potter

In memory of Joetta

This book is offered with love to every family whose life
has been temporarily devastated by a child's sexual molestation.
It is dedicated with great hope to the healing of those
courageous children and their grieving families.

It is also dedicated to my husband, Philip, and daughter, Susan.
Grateful thanks for your continued love and support.
—Kathryn Brohl

May this book encourage all parents who read it to vow they
will say to their abused child of any age, "It wasn't your fault"—
as many times as that child needs to hear it.
—Joyce Case Potter

When Your Child Has Been Molested

Learning Your Child Has Been Molested

Janet and Bill Thompson recently discovered that their son Scott had been molested. They were appalled and saddened by the idea that someone violated their child, nine-year-old Scott. Friendly and bright, Scott is a popular child who played Tom Sawyer in his class play, and with his red hair and freckles, he was well suited to the part. He loves the outdoors and enjoys building tree houses and forts with the other neighborhood kids.

The Thompsons feel numb and confused. They wonder why they couldn't prevent their son's abuse. Would Scott believe them when they said they would protect him from further harm? Was it a realistic promise? Why did their emotions swing so dramatically? And how were they to keep their seven-year-old daughter, Beth, safe? Had their seventeen-year-old son, Brad, been molested as well but was too afraid to let them know?

WHEN SCOTT FIRST DISCLOSED

Janet and Bill worked hard at being good parents and felt strongly about getting their children involved in activities that encouraged confidence building. Scott, who loved the outdoors, became a member of a youth camping program, much like the one Bill fondly remembered from his childhood.

For the first two years, Scott was enthusiastic about his program experience. He liked palling around with his friends and the outdoor activities. But recently, Janet and Bill had noticed his interest dwindling. He would forget meetings, or disappear when it was time to go, or say he didn't feel like going. A few times he said he was too old for "that camping stuff."

A few days ago, while father and son were painting the family's fishing boat, Bill asked Scott how his camping program was going. Scott replied by shyly asking his dad why people became gay. A little taken aback, Bill gently asked his son what had prompted the question. Scott replied that his friends thought their camping instructor, Mr. Webster, was gay.

Confused by his son's comments, Bill asked Scott to explain. Scott answered in a strained voice, saying that his leader made weird comments when they were alone and they made him feel nervous. Scott's dad quietly encouraged his son to continue, taking great pains to keep painting.

Mr. Webster told Scott he liked to see the boys with their clothes off because they seemed to be less stressed. He told them that most nature lovers wore little or no clothing. Scott went on to say that he averted Mr. Webster's stares and in close settings sometimes felt the older man's hand brush across his crotch.

Scott continued, saying that he no longer enjoyed the outings and wanted to withdraw from program activities. He didn't know what to make of an authority figure behaving in such strange ways. Confused, Scott feared he, Scott, was gay.

Bill held his emotions in check when he told his son that no one had a right to touch or speak to Scott in ways that made him feel uncomfortable. Mr. Webster had been wrong, and Scott had done nothing to encourage him. Bill thanked Scott for speaking to him and emphasized that Scott had done nothing wrong.

Later, Bill and Janet discreetly asked other program parents if their children had mentioned Mr. Webster's behavior. They were extremely careful not to make false accusations, but they wanted to know if Scott's experience was isolated or if other children had also been affected.

It was soon apparent that Scott's remarks were similar to those of some of the other young campers. Sometimes reluctantly and other times with relief, they disclosed their experiences. Then out of the blue, Scott shared another startling disclosure with his parents: Mr. Webster had fondled him.

The Thompsons were stunned by this surprising new information. They didn't know that children often begin by disclosing their abuse only partially. After they receive reassuring feedback, they feel safer to share their full experience.

Janet and Bill had never thought that anyone would sexually molest their children. And although they were sure their son had been harmed, they weren't sure what child sexual abuse actually meant.

The following reality check defines child sexual abuse. Keep in mind that the legal definition for child sexual assault varies from state to state.

Reality Check 1: Child Sexual Abuse Definition

Child sexual abuse is any act with a child or youth that is intended to sexually gratify an adult, and in certain cases another child or youth. Sexual activity can include but is not limited to clothed or unclothed exposure of genitalia, fondling, masturbation, intimate kissing, verbal discussion, anal or oral intercourse, or pornography exposure that is enacted with a minor by a person who holds power over the event.

Asking a child or youth to engage in sexual activity, *even if it does not occur,* is child sexual assault. Asking the child or youth to engage in sexual activities with animals or objects is sexual assault. And a person commits the offense of child molestation when he or she does any other sexually explicit act to or in the presence of or with any child or youth.

Physical contact with a child or youth is *not* required for conviction of child sexual abuse. Most states agree that child sexual abuse laws are designed to protect children from exploitation regardless of whether their participation was voluntary. (Specific descriptions of child sex crimes are given in the Additional Information section at the end of the book.)

WHO MOLESTS CHILDREN?

Janet and Bill were disturbed that Mr. Webster pretended to care about children but took advantage of his position. How would this situation affect the young campers? Would their experiences have an impact on their trust? In the future, how would they decide which situations were safe and which weren't? The Thompsons knew that when it came to their own child, they could not excessively restrict what they allowed Scott to do and still provide him with a normal childhood.

Certainly most people who work with children and youth do it for the right reasons. Yet people who molest children often place themselves in positions that put them in contact with young people. *Most sex offenders know their victims.* And sexual molestation may occur in a progressive way over time or happen only once.

The following reality check shares facts about child and youth sexual abuse, as well as child molesters. This information is not meant to raise your anxiety but to help with your understanding.

Reality Check 2: Facts That Challenge Misconceptions About Child Sexual Abuse and Child Molesters

> ✓ Intercourse is not necessary to constitute sexual abuse. (See Reality Check 1.)
>
> ✓ Children *do not* seduce adults.
>
> ✓ Sexual molestation has always occurred and continues to occur in all societies worldwide.
>
> ✓ A physical illness such as diabetes or cancer does not prompt child sexual abuse. In other words, it's not

prompted by disease unless it may be a severe mental illness.

✓ Most people are not insane when they molest children.

✓ Child molesters represent all age, economic, ethnic, social, racial, and religious groups. They can be geniuses, of normal intelligence, or intellectually slow.

✓ Child molesters are single, married, divorced, or separated. They are heterosexual, bisexual, or homosexual. And they can be male or female.

✓ There are different theories and a good deal of speculation, but no one really knows why sex offenders sexually abuse children.

✓ The majority of people who sexually abuse children know their victims.

✓ Many sex offenders do not molest only one time. And they may have molested one or a number of children several times.

✓ Some sexual offenders report using alcohol or drugs when they molest kids. This circumstance does not minimize or justify the sexual abuse.

✓ Infants through older teenagers are molested.

✓ Sexual molestation can be as devastating for teenagers as it is for younger children.

✓ The same attention should be paid to very young children as well as older youth when seeking help for their sexual abuse.

✓ Children and youth who are molested usually experience a freezing response within their bodies that can inhibit their ability to fight or resist their molesters. It's

unrealistic to expect kids to speak out or fight
when they are in this circumstance, although some
children do.

✓ Children can molest other children. Although the
intervention that occurs with them is different from
that of adult child molesters, their behavior should be
disrupted and at the very least clarified with a sexual
abuse investigation worker.

✓ Any child—friendly and outgoing, or shy and
withdrawn—can be the victim of sexual abuse. Bright
or slower children can be harmed.

✓ A growing number of women are being prosecuted for
child sexual assault.

✓ Many child molesters were molested themselves as
children, but the vast majority of molested children do
not grow up to be child sex offenders.

✓ Being molested by an adult of the same sex does not
mean that the child victim is or will be homosexual.

TYPES OF ADULT SEX OFFENDERS

Child molesters are generally classified as preferential or situational
child molesters:

Preferential child molesters are sexually aroused by children. There
are different types of preferential child molesters, but the two
dominant ones are pedophiles, who are compulsively sexually
drawn to prepubescent children, and hebophiles, who are
compulsively sexually drawn to postpubescent males.

Situational child molesters are not compulsively sexually drawn
to children, but will engage them in sexual acts for a variety

of reasons. They may have distorted sexual fantasies, for example, and molesting a child is a departure from their usual sex patterns, or their behavior may be related to stress.

Note that those who have not acted on their urges to speak about sexual matters to children or to coerce children into sexual acts are not child sex offenders, and not all child molesters are pedophiles. Also, molesters from both groups may admit eventually to having molested more children over a longer period than when they first disclosed.

People who molest kids are like everyone else in many ways. They have families and jobs and may hold prominent positions in the community. They represent varied professions: doctors, police officers, church representatives, teachers, youth leaders, coaches, construction workers, funeral directors, postal workers, and others. They are friendly and helpful, or shy and withdrawn. They can be your friends or neighbors. Many sex offenders come from backgrounds that reflect extreme levels of deprivation and oppression; others may come from good homes.

Sex offenders are generally limited in how they deal with stress. Their coping skills in working through stressful times or their ability to communicate with others to solve problems is often immature. Consequently they may bottle or exaggerate their emotions and behave impulsively. In addition, it's not unusual for some to use drugs or alcohol, and they may be physically and verbally abusive. Others feel empowered by having sexual contact with children. And some commit other crimes that indicate they do not feel remorse.

Rarely, some child molesters demonstrate extraordinary self-control, to the point of being rigid about their routines and even ritualistic in how they molest children. After their sexual assault, they may feel energized and even euphoric. Or they may feel intense remorse. They can also be overly controlling and critical in their other relationships. Preferential sex offenders are represented in this group.

Child molesters' personal lives are often troubled, and they may have a long, difficult history in forming and maintaining relationships. They may lack social skills, and their approach to sexual intimacy is concrete and may reflect thinking such as, "If he loves me, he'll have sex with me." And most rationalize (that is, justify) their behavior.

CHILDREN WHO MOLEST
OTHER CHILDREN

A growing number of child protection agencies are intervening with children who sexually molest other children. Child sexual molestation occurs when a child is used for another person's sexual gratification even if the molester is young.

Children frequently engage in normal experimental sexual behavior with each other, but some may have acquired more serious problems such as conduct or attachment disorders that reflect persistent violation of social norms with others. One of the characteristics of these conditions is to compulsively sexualize other kids, often with physical or verbal coercion. Children from severely deprived and abusive backgrounds living in environments where alcohol and illegal drugs are commonly used, war-torn countries, or violent communities can develop these disorders.

For example, a parent in Indiana was overwhelmed when her adopted son, raised for five years in another country, compulsively sexually abused his sister. Unable to stop her son's compulsive behavior, she felt helpless to protect her younger child and reported the abuse to the local child protection agency. Eventually the boy was removed from his home and placed in long-term therapeutic residential care.

Age doesn't necessarily make a difference in determining a sexual act by another child as abusive. A younger, more powerful child may use his ability to sexually abuse an older, more passive child such as one who is developmentally delayed.

Child Welfare Workers Had Worried About a Ten Year Old

Caseworkers had intervened for several years to try to sta-bilize a troubled boy. But when he was ten years old, he raped and then murdered another child. He lured a three year old away from a local library, sexually assaulted him, and left him to die. The mother of the murdered child was quoted as saying, "He shouldn't go to jail. He needs help. I know he has mental problems and if he goes to jail he'll just come out an angry adult."

Siblings and Other Family Members

In some situations, older siblings sexually indoctrinate younger kids. It may even be their cultural norm. But it's still wrong.

Siblings may target a particular brother or sister to sexually abuse. When she was a child, Sharon lived on a farm in Texas with her parents and two brothers. Her older brother, Bill, began to molest her when she was six years old. Because both of her parents were away working, she was terrified to spend time after school with Bill. She never knew if he would leave her alone or force her to engage in sexual acts. Sometimes he tied her to her bed. Other times he'd march her into the barn and coerce her into fondling animals. Sharon's parents were oblivious to the abuse, and she felt too frightened to let them know because Bill had threatened her on several occasions. As an adult, Sharon has difficulty trusting other people and even recognizing that her brother's behavior was rape. This is an example of domestic violence, which often gets ignored.

Bullies and Others Who Feel Empowered by Their Behaviors

Acquaintance rape is another way young people are being violated. With the escalating use of "club drugs" such as GHB, teenage females are unwittingly given beverages by "dates" that have been laced with these substances, leaving them helpless to defend themselves and even recall their sexual assault. (GHB is produced as an odorless, colorless liquid or white powder taken orally or combined with alcohol. It has been used as a date rape drug and produces sexual arousal, amnesia, nausea, drowsiness, respiratory distress, dizziness, and seizures.)

Bullies may coerce other youth into sexual activity. They also take advantage of other children in institutional settings such as group living centers or boarding schools. These types of situations are not always reported because victims may believe they'll get into trouble if they step forward to disclose what happened to them.

Child's Rape in School Went Undetected

One newspaper reported that four boys raped a twelve-year-old girl during school hours in the school's bathroom. Three other juveniles told police they witnessed the abuse but did not participate. Two of the rapists were twelve years old, one was thirteen, and another fourteen. The girl was found outside the bathroom by a friend after the attackers ran away. For over half an hour, none of these children were in class, yet their teachers did not notify the administration that the children were missing. Said the girl's mother, "She's afraid of going back to school. She's afraid. She's very afraid."

Child Sex Offenders Need Help

Child and adolescent sex offenders, especially younger children, may have suffered from previous traumatic experiences themselves. Often their behavior is a form of reenacting their own sexual abuse.

Nevertheless, these compulsive behaviors must be addressed through compassionate therapeutic interventions. Older youth need to be held responsible and court-ordered into therapy as well. Adults must interrupt the behavior and bring their child's sexual assault by a minor to the attention of child protective services. (The definition of *minor child* varies by state, but its upper range can extend from sixteen to nineteen years of age.) Otherwise, the sexual abuse incidents may occur more frequently or become more intense and serious.

Adult Sex Offender Registration, Interventions, and Other Sex Offender Definitions

- All those who have been found guilty of sexual abuse by a court of law are now required by law to register at their local law enforcement agency. They are also required to register their DNA.

- Megan's Law, important sex offender registration legislation, and the *Diagnostic and Statistical Manual of Mental Health Disorders* description of exhibitionism and pedophilia are described at the end of the book in the Additional Information section.

- Interventions being used with sex offenders include pharmacological and psychotherapy treatments, relapse prevention, court-ordered living restrictions, and prison terms.

LEARNING ABOUT YOUR CHILD'S ABUSE

Bill and Janet were grateful that Scott came to them first when he disclosed his experience. They realized how embarrassed and anxious he must have been. The Thompsons were fortunate their son shared his abuse with them first because caregivers often learn about their children's experience from other sources.

One of the more shocking ways to learn about your child's abuse is to witness the act or hear about it from an eyewitness. One mom reported feeling practically immobilized when she walked into a room and saw an older neighbor girl performing oral sex on her son. Another caregiver stated she had trouble believing her nephew when he described watching a teenage babysitter tongue-kissing her five-year-old niece.

Molested children often disclose their abuse to someone they think won't overreact to the information. They may talk to a day care worker or a teacher because they might first learn about inappropriate touching and wrong adult behavior in day care or at school. By sharing their experience with a safe person, they may be checking to see if they've done something wrong and if they're still okay.

A child may mention his sexual abuse during casual play or, having already been instructed about wrong touch, may disclose it in a small group setting. Depending on his age, he may share aloud or write about it in a poem. Sometimes children give nonverbal cues through their changed behavior and reveal their abuse only after direct questioning.

Astute teachers and other caregivers may spot abuse markers in a child's drawings or sudden destructive anger or during a routine medical exam. These indicators may lead them to ask questions. At other times, classmates or other friends may report another student's "different" actions to their own parents, prompting parent involvement.

It's not uncommon for child protection agencies to receive their initial complaint from a favorite relative who was drawn into the child's disclosure during a visit or telephone conversation. The Internet and cell phones make extended family members more accessible to children who have been sexually abused.

Parents may feel hurt if their children initially share their disclosures with others. One mother explained, "I felt I was a bad mother because she told someone else. I was guilt-ridden."

Child Sexual Abuse Statistics

- The average victim of child sexual abuse is between eight and eleven years old.

- One of four girls and one of six boys under the age of eighteen are victims.

- Incest is the most common form of sexual abuse.

- Current reports reflect that the majority of abusers are men.

- The average reported duration of abuse is one to four years. Abuse can continue over a longer time or occur once.

- Approximately 13 percent of all types of child abuse are determined to be sexual abuse. Children may suffer multiple forms of child abuse, which include child neglect and physical or emotional abuse.

Children may not tell their parents first because they are afraid of their parents' reactions. They worry that they will not be believed, or will be blamed or even punished, or that their parents will seek revenge. In fact, when their molestation occurs, they may have been in a forbidden place—somewhere their parents would not allow them to go. If a child has been abused at a neighbor's and he has been repeatedly warned about being there, he may be extremely reluctant to disclose that he went there. Parents must be clear that while they're not pleased about their child's disobedience, it didn't cause the molestation. The child is not responsible for his sexual abuse.

Children's fears are usually tied to their fear of caregiver abandonment as well as their own intellectual development. Because

being self-involved is part of normal child development, a child may
believe he is bad because of the bad things that happen in his life.
He may worry about burdening an already burdened parent. In addition, he may be frightened that his molester will return to harm him
or other family members.

Older children want to be viewed as normal, and they worry
about being labeled crazy or gay. Many youth resist drawing attention to themselves and believe they can handle their own problems.

More times than not, kids' fears are not founded and do not
reflect their parents' actual ability to deal with the information. Personal shame is a feeling that often develops in children who have
been molested. Children report that they fear their parents will feel
ashamed of them as well.

Don't be surprised if guilt begins to dominate your experience.
It's normal to feel guilt in response to hearing about your child's
experience. You may think you "should have been there" or "able

---

Understanding Shame

Webster's New World College Dictionary defines shame as
the absence of experiencing grace or a feeling of falling
from grace.

Children often feel shame as a result of their sexual
abuse. They feel as though they've personally lost something divine.

Shame can be positive, as a marker reminding us to
notice and correct behavior, or negative, as a trigger
that elicits feelings of being flawed or devalued. Where
there has been sexual assault, human shame develops
negatively.

Without appropriate intervention, repeatedly feeling
negative shame subsequently affects a child's self-perception
and worldview.

to prevent it." And you might be surprised to learn that some of your anger is connected with guilt.

Regardless, you must continue to communicate with your child and try not to allow your anger or guilt to stand in the way of future communication.

However you become aware of your child's molestation, give him the support and love he needs. You must all work together as you begin the child and family recovery process.

Chapter Two discusses how to make a report and handle this extremely sensitive information.

2

Reporting Child Sexual Abuse
Investigation and Prosecution Stages

J anet hung up the phone in tears. She had just reported her son's
molestation to the child abuse hot line. Having no experience or
other preparation, she and Bill were very unsure what to expect.

Later that evening, she and Bill explained to Scott that reporting the abuse was necessary to protect him and his friends from further harm, as well as hold Mr. Webster accountable for his actions.
(Chapter Three discusses what you can say to your child in order to
relieve her fears.)

After the children were in bed, Janet shared her worry with Bill
about what Scott and other family members would experience during and following the investigation. With whom they would speak
and would Mr. Webster be charged with child sexual abuse? How
many people would interview Scott, and would he be upset by their
questions? Would Mr. Webster be arrested, and would their names
be in the newspaper? In spite of these worries, Janet knew they had
done the right thing to report her son's sexual abuse.

OVERCOMING YOUR FEARS AND
REPORTING THE ABUSE

It's shocking to learn about your child's molestation. It can trigger a
grief response that feels similar to losing a loved one. An instinct to
reject outside help may be strong. Often, families want to "circle the

wagons" and isolate themselves to the extent that they don't discuss the sexual abuse even with other family members. You should resist the temptation to remain silent. Consider the fact that if a child molester is not stopped, his likelihood of molesting your child again or other children is high. People who compulsively sexually abuse children seldom stop without intervention.

You may not want to go beyond expressing concern and calming your child's fears, but your child's recovery requires outside help. In addition, you have an ethical, moral, and legal obligation to report the abuse.

When There Is Community Pressure

You may be faced with a difficult decision if you live in a community that sends a different message. For example, many immigrant or other insular societies such as religious sects settle disputes within their communities. For a number of reasons, then, asking for outside help, especially from the dominant culture, is discouraged. If your neighbors and friends see your accessing outside help for your child and family as a community betrayal, this situation can leave you in a quandary.

One Native American child welfare worker reported that working with conventional tribal protocol in sexual abuse matters can be extremely sensitive. And a Vietnamese worker stated that he can bridge the communication gap between Western and Eastern cultures when he uses the help of elders within his community.

Culturally aware workers are becoming more sensitive in these environments, but they need support. Remember that sexual abuse affects all children because it goes beyond their understanding and can create serious psychological problems for them in the future. In addition, not reporting sexual abuse is against the law.

Your Team of Helpers

The professionals who intervene on behalf of sexually abused children include child protection workers, officers of the court such as police and prosecuting attorneys, an examining physician, and counselors or therapists. A licensed counseling professional is required by law to call the abuse hot line. And all states require professionals who work directly with children, such as teachers and child care workers, to report their suspicions about child abuse. Many states also require citizens to report suspected abuse as well. *It is vitally important to report the abuse.*

WHAT HAPPENS NEXT? THE INVESTIGATION AND PROSECUTION STAGES

The investigation and prosecution stages described here may not be exactly what you experience because child sexual abuse investigations and prosecutions vary by state. Although most protocols are similar, each case is different. Don't let these stages overwhelm or discourage you. Having this information will make this experience less frustrating and reduce your family's anxiety.

The process begins with a phone call to the state or local child abuse hot line. The hot line may be connected to a law enforcement office or to child protective services, or it can be connected to a larger central monitoring location that calls the local services. The number is published in your local phone book, usually in the emergency section in the first few pages. If your call is an emergency and your child is in danger, phone 911.

Calling in a false report is subject to prosecution.

Stage One

The person recording your report will ask you questions, so it's helpful to write down the specifics before you call. Write down dates, identifying descriptions, times, and anything else that you think will help investigators do their job. You will be told that within a certain period of time, the report will be investigated. Times frames generally range from immediately to twenty-four hours. The hot line worker will note the severity of the report and if there is risk to the child by virtue of sharing a residence with the alleged perpetrator. Your report will likely be recorded, so don't add comments such as, "If someone doesn't respond soon, I'm going to take matters into my own hands." Such comments confuse investigators and can trigger unnecessary police involvement.

Stage Two

If the police or sheriff's department uses a child protection service such as a special child sexual abuse unit, it will be called in to act as consultants to law enforcement. This service may offer facilities and skills that enhance the processing of the investigation. Sometimes law enforcement requests that callers directly telephone the special child protection sexual assault unit.

Law enforcement will wish to include the child protection service in the investigation process, particularly if the alleged offender is a family member. "Family members" include extended family, someone to whom the parents have entrusted the care of their child, dangerous environments that are repeatedly used for care, and parents' boyfriends or girlfriends.

Some parts of the country also include the help of a child protection team, also called a child advocacy center, which is a specialized team of child assault professionals that offers a range of assistance, including interview space, pediatric examinations, and victim advocacy.

Stage Three

Each state requires workers to speak face to face with the child within a certain time frame, depending on the severity of the allegation and risk to the child. The first meeting is to substantiate the report and decide if there is cause to believe that a sexual assault has occurred. This meeting is often brief and usually takes place in a neutral setting, such as a school, or parents may be asked to bring their child to the agency's office. Workers may also visit the child's home if the alleged offender is not residing there.

Stage Four

If a determination has been made that further investigation is needed, the police officer or detective and/or protective service worker will arrange a time with the child's parents or primary caregiver to interview the child in a more formal setting for a forensic interview or examination/evaluation. Arrangements may also be made to examine the child for physical trauma and evaluate her overall physical condition. Examinations are utilized when a child has disclosed abuse or her history points to a strong suspicion of physical trauma. Most communities have special pediatric units designed specifically to examine child abuse victims, where specially trained doctors examine the children. Do not have your child examined by your family physician unless the investigation team gives its approval.

The formal or forensic interview may take place at the law enforcement agency, the offices of your state or county child protective agency, or the offices of an assisting consultative agency contracted to do child abuse investigations within your community. Your child's interview may be videotaped to preserve the child's disclosure. (If your child is young, let her know that she is not on television and will not be on any of the television channels.)

Stage Five

If the alleged offender is living in your home, he or she may be asked to leave the house following the formal interview. If the alleged perpetrator refuses to leave, the nonoffending parent or guardian will be asked to leave the home with the child. If neither of these arrangements is possible or if the nonoffending parent is unable to protect the child, the youngster could be temporarily placed in what is determined to be a safe environment. A safe environment may be relative, non-relative, or institutional placement. By law, there is generally a hearing soon (usually within forty-eight hours) after any out-of-home placement. At this hearing, the child protection agency must justify to the court why this was necessary. The court then decides the child's most appropriate placement.

Stage Six

After the interview (and examination if one is needed), the police official and other agency personnel will decide if the information obtained justifies referral to a prosecuting attorney, who is a state criminal justice official. The prosecuting attorney will speak with the investigators, view the videotape, and make a judgment on whether to bring a criminal action against the alleged child molester. (All references to court in this book pertain to criminal court.)

You may be asked to refrain from speaking with the media or talking with other victims' families for the time being. Reasons may vary, but there is usually sound logic behind this request, and you should cooperate.

Stage Seven

The state prosecuting attorney determines whether or not to file criminal charges against the alleged perpetrator. This decision is based on a number of factors, the strongest being the believability of the child's disclosure, including the medical evidence.

Stage Eight

If charges are filed, a warrant is sworn out for the arrest of the alleged perpetrator.

Stage Nine

The person is arrested if located and read his or her rights. An offer to take a lie detector test (polygraph) is usually made if the alleged offender denies the allegations. Many people decline, especially if they have legal representation. Lie detector results are not admissible in court, but failure to pass one may strengthen the prosecution's motivation to prosecute the case.

The alleged offender's denial is understandable. If the victim's story is believed, the offender has a good deal to lose, including likely rejection by immediate and extended family and friends and jeopardized professional standing and employment. An offender found guilty of child sexual misconduct will be placed on probation or go to prison.

The psychological consequences of admitting guilt can be overwhelming because sex offenders are usually ashamed of their acts. Many sex offenders have developed their own complex rationalization systems over years. They can lie convincingly and may call on their family or friends to provide character references and support. Enthusiastic testimonies have been provided by people who truly believed a molester's claim of innocence.

Stage Ten

Within a period mandated by law, an alleged offender must be brought before a judge or magistrate (a civil officer of the court empowered to administer the law) to determine whether there is probable cause to support the arrest. If probable cause is found, the judge sets bond at a monetary amount or holds the defendant over without bond. When paid, bond allows the defendant to be released until the trial. A defendant who is held over without bond goes to jail to await trial.

At this time, the defendant is given an arraignment date for the next court appearance. This may occur in a few days or several weeks, depending on the court schedule, or *docket*.

Before the arraignment hearing, the defendant and his or her attorney may consent to a prefiling agreement in which the defense and prosecuting attorney negotiate a plea and recommend a penalty. For example, the defendant may agree to plead "no contest," an admission that the charges are not denied. This may be done in exchange for the prosecution's recommendation to the court that the offender be placed on probation and court-ordered into a sex offenders' treatment program.

The judge will consider the plea and prefiling agreement rec-ommendations at the arraignment hearing. If they are accepted, a sentencing date will be set.

Stage Eleven

An arraignment hearing occurs regardless of whether there is a pre-filing agreement. At the arraignment, the defendant appears before a judge to hear the charges and plead guilty or not guilty. More than likely, the defendant will have an attorney, who will waive (give up voluntarily) the reading of the information and plead not guilty on behalf of the defendent. This may be done in hopes of negotiating an agreement on these charges at a later time.

A defendant who has not acquired an attorney will be advised to do so. A court-appointed lawyer from the public defender's office may be appointed if the defendant is unable to pay for legal services.

If no prefiling agreement has been decided, a trial date is set at the arraignment hearing. The court's schedule and also the consti-tutional right to a speedy trial determine the trial date.

Stage Twelve

After the arraignment hearing, the defendant's attorney has the right to file a demand for discovery. This means that all of the pros-ecution evidence against the alleged perpetrator must be made available to the defense team—for example, names of witnesses, copies of witnesses' statements, and a taped or written copy of the child's interview.

The defense may also contact the prosecuting attorney and try to negotiate a sentencing agreement. For instance, the defense lawyer might say, "My client acknowledges his mistake and has started counseling." The prosecuting attorney will contact the child's guardians to determine if they would be open to bypassing a trial and negotiating the sentence now. However, the legal right to make a final determination remains with the court.

Stage Thirteen

Shortly before the trial date, a *docket sounding*—a conference between the judge and defense and prosecuting attorneys—occurs.
This meeting is held so that the attorneys announce their readiness
for trial. If they are not prepared, they must give reasons.

It's not unusual to extend, or *continue*, the trial date, allowing
additional time for preparation. If the date is continued and the
delay is caused by the defense, the defense may waive the defendant's right to a speedy trial. These cases might not come to trial
until months after charges are filed against the alleged offender.
(Further discussion follows in Chapters Seven and Fourteen, respec-
tively, about why the legal process can take time as well as how to
prepare your child to appear in court.)

Stage Fourteen

If the defendant is found guilty, a sentencing date will be set. If the
alleged offender is found not guilty, the case will be closed and there
will be no more activity in criminal court.

TYPES OF COURTS

The stages described in this chapter refer to criminal court. Criminal court actions are taken when the state brings charges against an
alleged child sex offender. Most states provide specific court divi-
sions for resolving issues involving children. There are three other
courts that a family could be involved with in a child sexual abuse
case, which may be generally described as follows:

Probate or juvenile court, which rules on issues dealing with protecting children. Child protection agencies responsible for child
welfare gain temporary protective custody and decide child visitation issues in juvenile court.

Family court, which rules on cases where the alleged molestation is linked with divorce or disputed custody or when visitation issues arise.

Civil court, which rules on personal injury when lawsuits are filed by families of victims or the victim against perpetrators or negligent child advocacy agents.

It's possible, though unlikely, that families could be involved with all four court systems simultaneously.

TAKING THAT FIRST STEP

You take a very courageous and necessary step when you notify the authorities after your child's sexual assault. Janet and Bill were protecting their son when they contacted the child abuse hot line. Although they were not certain, they intuitively felt that if Mr. Webster were found guilty of molesting their son, he may be stopped from harming other children.

The following chapters will help you understand what happens next and support you and your family as you work through your feelings and proceed through the legal process.

3

Supporting Your Child
After His Disclosure

No matter how you learn about your child's molestation, your reaction to the information is very important in determining how your family will eventually heal. Your child needs your continuing reassurance because he may feel responsible for his experience and guilty for disclosing. (Remember that with help, children do work through their abuse and go on to work, play, and love.)

After you've made the report to the local child abuse hot line, you must demonstrate to your child by your words and actions that you will protect him from further harm. You need to reassure him through a variety of ways—for example.

- Appreciating his courage to disclose

- Removing him from a dangerous environment

- Continuing to be supportive

- Limiting the number of people he tells until the investigation has been completed

YOUR FIRST RESPONSE

Your first response after hearing about your child's abuse is crucial. He will likely observe your body language and listen to your verbal cues signaling he has done nothing wrong. Negative responses can be strongly registered in your child and may affect your relationship.

Here are some do's and don'ts guidelines:

• *Don't* respond negatively to your child's disclosure. Comments such as, "How could you be so stupid? You must be imagining things!" or "Why didn't you try to stop him?" are not helpful and can potentially retraumatize a child. Other inappropriate remarks that send a judgmental message, such as, "You're ruined!" or "You're marked for life!" can confuse younger kids. They may wonder where their bodies are marked and if other people will notice.

• *Don't* sweep the incident under the rug by telling your child that you'll handle the situation alone. It is a mistake not to make a report. Here is one woman's story.

Maria's Story

Maria, now an adult, remembers that when she was nine years old, she told her parents about her uncle's sexual abuse. They said they would handle the situation and directed her not to tell anyone else. Her parents didn't make a report or discuss her sexual assault with her ever again. They probably felt that bringing up the abuse would upset Maria, but their good intentions backfired. Maria grew up believing there was something wrong with her because she had to keep the abuse secret. She had no clue about what would happen and was not told how the situation was handled. She was terrified when she saw her uncle at family reunions and never knew how her parents had dealt with the situation other than that they stopped visiting his house.

• *Do* allow your child to lead the sexual assault discussion. Answer his questions and comments according to his age and ability to understand. Most five year olds, for example, don't need a lot of explanation. Try to respond simply, in twenty-five words or less. An older child may ask questions, and you can both look up answers together.

• *Don't* discuss more than your child can handle. Remember that children generally give you signals when they want to end the discussion. They'll ask about their soccer practice perhaps or turn on the television. And protect your child from unnecessary information regarding his case.

• *Do* keep to your child's regular routine. Routines help children feel safe and settle their anxiety. Providing consistency during this crisis will help him feel calmer.

• *Don't* threaten to harm the alleged perpetrator. When children hear well-meaning adults threaten to physically harm the alleged child molester, it can raise their fear about being targeted by their assailant. They can be afraid they will be punished for disclosing. If the alleged perpetrator has threatened to harm his parents, a child may be reluctant to disclose as well. This is natural if he has been threatened. He may also worry about his parents' being arrested and sent to jail if they harm the alleged perpetrator.

• *Do* control your emotions around your children. Your feelings, while understandable, should be kept in check around all your kids. Children can feel extremely responsible if their parents seem fragile or otherwise unable to cope. Take pains not to place your child in an inappropriate caretaking role. And do not unconsciously turn your child off by acting as though you are embarrassed or are otherwise overwhelmed by the disclosure.

• *Don't* ask leading questions or put your child in an embarrassing position. For example, if your child makes a disclosure, you can gently ask him to continue by saying, "Go on" or "What would you like me to know?" But never say, especially with younger children, something like, "Did he take his hand and cover your mouth, and did you try and scream?" Or "Did it feel good?" In doing so you could affect your child's credibility with investigators because he may unconsciously insert this information into his disclosure when he is interviewed. It may lead investigators to conclude that he has been prompted or coached.

Recent neural research has discovered that under certain circumstances and with certain individuals, false memories can be implanted in people. (There is more on false memory research in the Additional Information section.) So what you say to your child after his disclosure is vitally important. You don't want your remarks to be judged by the investigators as coaching. Do not ask unnecessary questions, and control your reactions.

• *Do* allow the professionals to do the investigative work. Your job is to support your child. It will help the professionals if you've jotted down his remarks when he first disclosed and share the information with them.

RESPONDING TO YOUR CHILD

After your child discloses his abuse, thank him, stressing that it was the right thing for him to do. The reality check that follows gives you some more suggestions.

Reality Check 3: What to Say to Your Child

✓ "I am glad you told me. I know this wasn't easy. Thank you."

✓ "You are very brave and did the right thing by telling me. I know it may not have been easy, but you need to know that you didn't do anything wrong."

✓ "We know how scary this may have been for you to talk to us. This is a problem we need help with, and there are special people who can be helpful."

✓ "I'm sorry I wasn't there to stop this from happening. It wasn't your fault. We're going to talk to some people who will help us."

✓ "You are very brave, and the person who hurt you was wrong! We're here for you."

✓ "You are smart to talk to me. I'm really proud of you. Now we need to tell somebody who can help us. There are people who know how to work with this kind of situation."

✓ "I am so proud of you for letting me handle this situation. The thing I need to do now is make a report to people who know how to stop [the alleged perpetrator]."

✓ "Thank you for telling me. Is there anything I can do to help you feel better?"

It is important that your child know from the start that his team of helping professionals has a job to do. At times, you may feel that they are not supporting your child or family adequately and may even be giving the alleged perpetrator the benefit of the doubt. However, don't telegraph any of this anger or frustration to your child. And let him know that talking to helpers as well as appearing in court is not punishment. Although it may be difficult, it is part of getting through the experience.

BELIEVING YOUR CHILD

Mild-mannered Mr. Webster didn't fit the profile that Janet and Bill Thompson had in mind for a child sex offender—a profile that was based on movies and other stereotypical ideas. The soft-spoken program leader was in his sixties and married, with grown children.

Assessing a child's believability can be confusing because children do lie at times. It's a natural part of their psychological development. Sometimes young children make up stories based on fairy tales or imaginary friends. It's normal for parents who encourage their child to use his imagination to doubt the believability of his disclosure, especially if it's intertwined with "pretend" characters. However, children seldom disclose information if they have no knowledge about it. For example a child will generally not disclose that a teacher put her finger in his "poopie" if he hasn't had the experience, he hasn't been coached, or he hasn't seen or heard about it from another source such as an adult video or another child. Because children this young seldom disclose this type of information, it needs further investigation.

Older children lie when they're afraid of being punished for something they did or didn't do. For instance, eleven-year-old Jeb told his parents that he had finished all of his chores when he finished only half of them. And sixteen-year-old Jennifer may tell her parents she's staying overnight at a friend's house when she's really going to a party. But unless there are extenuating problems, most teenagers do not make up their sexual abuse experiences. An adolescent may tell a close friend about an acquaintance rape and then deny anything happened when later asked by her parents. Some disclose after years of abuse and only when they fear that a younger sibling will be the perpetrator's next target. In addition, teenagers who have been sexually active may fear they will be labeled "sluts" or "whores" or blamed if they reveal a sexual assault by an adult such as a stepparent.

If parents have trouble believing their child's disclosure, they need to keep their doubts to themselves, at least until an investigation has been completed. In any case, it is their parental obligation to report the abuse.

Common sense dictates the direction that parents should take. For example, if their small child tells them that a baby-sitter touched his "privates" during bath time, parents need to find out if the caregiver was attempting to wash their child. Of course, they'll want to check for any physical trauma. But if there are no signs of trauma, they should ask the baby-sitter to let them take care of bathing. Or if a teenager reports a sexual assault but has reported unsubstantiated sexual assaults in the past, parents might question him *and* refer him to a sexual abuse specialist for counseling yet still make a report.

In some custody or divorce situations, young children have been coached into believing that they've been sexually molested by one of the parents. Sometimes they *have* been molested by one of the parents. These cases are extremely complex and can be extraordinarily confusing. The best approach is to report the disclosure, and let the investigators do their job.

CHILDREN AND SEXUAL ABUSE REPORTS

Children seldom lie about being molested. Most of the time they have no reason to lie or lack the intellectual capability to do so. In addition, their experience may leave them feeling exposed, ashamed, and just plain "icky." Other times, confused by their body's natural sexual arousal in response to being fondled or kissed, they will blame themselves and clam up. Telling someone about an assault can trigger them into reexperiencing the abuse and reinforce their bad feelings. (Children are often traumatized by their abuse, and avoidance behavior is one trauma symptom.)

By virtue of the fact that adults can be intimidating, kids may keep their abuse secret, especially when they are threatened. Ten-year-old Tracy's stepfather told her that if she told anyone about his molesting her, she would be sent to jail. One sex offender threatened to kill a small girl's pet rabbits if she disclosed. The child became obsessed with placing the animals nearby, and when her mother complained of their smell, the little girl became alarmed, asking if her rabbits were going to be "murdered."

The threat doesn't need to be dire. One child molester told his victim he could watch him with his X-ray vision. Another said that their contact was something special because the victim was special.

Children and youth almost never divulge their abuse to cause problems. One of their dominant fears relates to their anxiety about being blamed if they disclose. Consequently, it can be extremely difficult for them to report their experience.

Sometimes parents actually reject a child who has disclosed abuse. This happened to Ann.

Ann's Story

Fifteen-year-old Ann lived with her mother and stepfather. She hadn't had an easy childhood because her family moved around a lot, and she had little contact with her biological father.

Ann's mother worked nights as a nurse, and Ann was responsible for getting her younger brother and sister fed and put to bed. Before marrying her step-father, Ann's mom had struggled to pay bills and fight depression. Ann, drawn into a caretaking role, felt responsible for the family.

After her mother married Greg, the family's living conditions improved. There was money for school clothes and even occasional vacations. But soon after the marriage, Ann became bothered by Greg's behavior. After she put the other kids to bed, he would invite her to have a beer or compliment her on her figure. Sometimes he would be viewing a pornographic video when she walked into the family room. Other times, under the guise of asking her about her day, he would walk into her bedroom as she was undressing.

Then he began to hug her in less than fatherly ways, and finally, he held and fondled her breasts as she stood at the kitchen sink. His come-from-behind behavior startled and scared Ann.

Because her mother's depression had seemed to disappear after the marriage and she and Greg had even mentioned buying a house, Ann felt torn. She managed to contain her stepfather's behavior by locking her bedroom door and being unavailable in the evenings. But when she noticed Greg getting friendlier with her younger sister, she became alarmed.

She reported her abuse to a favorite teacher. She hoped her mother wouldn't blame her for what happened, but she was wrong. After being contacted by child protective services, Ann's mom became enraged; she said that Greg was just trying to be a good father and Ann was responsible for making the family go hungry, and she insinuated that Ann had encouraged Greg's advances. Her mother's response was devastating to Ann. Soon Ann withdrew, or *recanted*, her story. (Children may withdraw or recant their abuse disclosures because they are threatened or fear abandonment by their caregivers. Many times they are trying to please a nonoffending parent. Recanting is just one victimization stage and is part of a series of stages called Child Accommodation Syndrome.)

Fortunately, the workers at child protective services were diligent in their investigation and able to prosecute Greg. But much of the damage for Ann had been done. In therapy later, Ann understood she'd done the right thing, but as an adult, she has a strained relationship with her mother and never leaves her own children alone with their grandmother.

MR. WEBSTER'S SEDUCTION

Mr. Webster threaded his sexual abuse into the camping experience. He subtly coerced the boys to take their clothes off by having contests and promising rewards. First establishing a pleasant fatherly relationship, he gained the children's trust, so it didn't occur to them that he would have anything but the best of intentions. When he touched them, it was just part of becoming a man, he explained. And they complied.

Webster was doing what many child molesters do: slowly escalating a seduction. By first engaging a child in play or discussion, a molester may gradually expose him to more intense sexual experiences. This process does not necessarily involve threats, force, or strong-arm tactics, and the abuse doesn't always end with sexual intercourse. The following reality check discusses a child molestation progression that follows a familiar sex offender pattern.

Reality Check 4: The Progression of Seduction

After engaging a child's trust or becoming familiar in some way, a perpetrator may demonstrate any of the following behaviors:

- ✓ He begins to make comments or engages the child in more intimate interaction, with comments such as, "Did anyone ever tell you you were a very soft little girl?" or "I bought you your favorite ice cream, but I want to play a game first."

- ✓ Then or a little later, the perpetrator may wear loose-fitting clothes and expose or touch various parts of his own body.

- ✓ Watching a pornographic video together can be part of the seduction. The abuser may show pornographic pictures as well.

✓ The perpetrator may touch his body first by masturbating or with a child on his lap begin rubbing a hand across the child's genitals. Children report that they notice the abuser's breathing change.

✓ A perpetrator may ask the child to touch his penis, or a female perpetrator will place a child's hand on her breast. (In recent years, more young men have reported sexual abuse by women. Long overlooked, this topic is now coming to the light and given appropriate attention. Do not minimize the impact of sexual abuse by females on young males.)

✓ Sometimes the seduction escalates when perpetrators simulate intercourse (dry intercourse) by rubbing their genitals against a child's body, between legs or buttocks, or in the vaginal or anal area. There is no actual penetration.

✓ These behaviors can eventually lead to more intense sexual contact and may include touching of the vulva, hymen, anus, and vagina using a finger, the lip, or the tongue. Sometimes objects are used. Sexual intercourse may follow.

✓ After the molestation, child molesters may not say anything, threaten the child not to tell, or offer a reward.

———

When child molesters are strangers, behavior such as rape may escalate more quickly. And children may be asked to participate in ritualistic behavior during their abuse, such as donning robes, lighting candles, or speaking certain words.

OTHER TYPES OF SEXUAL
ASSAULT WITH CHILDREN

Assault by Strangers

Sexual assault by strangers occurs less often than it does with people the child knows. When it happens, it can be brutal and swift. Sexual abuse by strangers can even happen where children seem safe. For example, two sisters in a southern state were playing in a field behind their beautiful new home. The developers had used safety as a selling point to attract buyers, and the parents of these children had bought the sales pitch.

The girls, ages seven and ten, were unaware of the man on the bicycle watching them. They were surprised when they heard him ask them to come over and help him fix his bike. Shyly, they walked over to the man.

He swiftly grabbed the youngest child and told her sister that he would kill her if the older one didn't take her clothes off. Then tearing off a tree limb while holding the younger child, he proceeded to strike the ten year old on her buttocks. Afterward, he directed the children to lie down on the ground and count to one thousand while he left the scene.

The two children counted and then got up. The older girl dressed, and they walked home. The experience was surreal and confusing. Years later, the girls reported that they were deeply affected by the assault, but especially grateful that their parents believed them when they disclosed the assault.

Sexual Assault via the Internet

The Internet is becoming a vehicle for child molesters to meet children on-line, and the consequences can be frightening. For example, one thirteen-year-old sixth grader was strangled by her assailant in a mall parking lot after they'd connected through an Internet chatroom.

The Crimes Against Children Research Center (CCRC) at the University of New Hampshire studied this trend in sexual abuse and concluded that compared with other young people who are molested, sexual assault through the Internet is less common. Nevertheless, it's estimated that kids run at least a 20 percent chance of being targeted by a sexual predator on-line for the purpose of engaging in sexual contact later on.

Lack of good data also makes this a difficult topic to assess. David Finkelhor, director of CCRC, has been quoted saying that sexual offenses against young people through the Internet are generally underreported. Parents may have no idea that their child is meeting someone dangerous when he uses the computer. The on-line seduction occurs something like this:

1. The perpetrator establishes communication.

2. The perpetrator evaluates a child's vulnerability and identifies him as a target.

3. Personal or pornographic photos may be traded between them.

4. The perpetrator begins to engage in cybersex, or sex on-line, with the child by using sexually explicit language and proposing greater communication or contact.

5. Phone conversations are initiated, which lead to phone sex.

6. A face-to-face meeting is arranged for the purpose of physically molesting the child.

Kidnapping and Rape

Reports of child and youth kidnapping and rape have been sensationalized in the media. In some instances, children have been murdered. On rare occasions, they have been kidnapped and later became victims of the Stockholm syndrome. (The name is taken from an adult kidnapping incident that occurred in the city of Stockholm, Sweden, where the victims began to bond with their captors.)

For example, a young girl who has been kidnapped by an older man may be targeted as her abductor's prospective "wife." As time goes by, she begins to build a relationship with her kidnappers.

The Stockholm syndrome develops as the child feels gratitude for being spared from death and then gradually gets caught up in his captor's story. Many people have wondered why these victims become so attached to their kidnappers that when opportunities for escape occur, they don't leave. It can be psychologically impossible for the young person to leave his captors.

WHEN CHILDREN ARE NOT SUPPORTED

Normal psychological as well as physical development can be disrupted when children and youth are molested. Often, an anxious condition within the child develops. This condition is expressed through a number of characteristics or symptoms described in Chapter Four, but for the most part, they can be mended when there is early therapeutic intervention and strong parental support. The following reality check describes the psychological fallout that can occur when a child or youth is not believed.

Sexually Abused Females

It is estimated that approximately 80 percent of adult women with drug or alcohol addictions were sexually molested in childhood.

Reality Check 5: What Can Happen If You Don't Support Your Child

✓ His confidence can be deeply affected.

Sara's parents thought she was making it up when, at age twelve, she disclosed her grandfather's sexual abuse. He'd been molesting her for two years, and she wanted it to stop. Her parents couldn't believe that her dad's father was capable of "such a thing" because he was a prominent community figure and extremely generous in financially supporting the family. Her parents thought that Sara's low self-esteem and moodiness had more to do with her age, not her grandfather. Sara was told she was ungrateful and stretching her imagination because she had probably mistaken her grandfather's demonstration of affection for something else. Later, Sara's disclosure was validated when her ten-year-old cousin divulged that their grandfather had started molesting her too.

✓ His ability to trust is affected.

Trust develops when repeated experiences let a child know his parents are reliable caretakers. Trust begins developing when infants are aroused to cry as a response to their hunger. If their cries for basic needs are met, they naturally move to another trust level. Children's ability to trust can be affected by spotty or negligent caretaking, which can create problems later when it comes to trusting other people. When children aren't supported following their sexual assault, they lose trust in the people who should be advocating for them.

✓ He may acquire distorted thinking.

He may feel he is invisible to his caregivers and begin to believe, "If I'm not believed, how can I be important?" Consequently, his ability to assert himself can be limited because he may assume his feelings and opinions will be ignored.

✓ He may dissociate, or remove himself mentally from the experience.

This response later when he is under stress may cause him to "check out," or become distracted, at school or in other areas of their life. If no one is there to take care of his problem, he may develop an alter or another personality that allows him to disconnect mentally from the molestation. This is called Altered Personality Disorder.

✓ He may have a difficult time forming relationships.

The thinking of adults who have not been believed about their childhood molestation may run along the lines of waiting for "the other shoe to drop" and can compel them to avoid getting close to other people.

For example, Jeff was molested from ages six to nine by his piano teacher. He had practiced detaching himself from feeling anything pleasurable during these experiences. Now age forty, he has learned to approach sex from a less-than-intimate manner, basically viewing his partners as objects. Never married, he "arranges" for his sexual encounters and lives a lonely life.

✓ He may develop magical thinking, another form of distorted thinking.

Wishful thinking can help a child cope with the experience. For example, he may think of himself as a Power Ranger with the ability to disappear. Or she may believe her life will dramatically change when she has her own baby. Magical thinking may last a lifetime and inhibits someone from coping with life's realities and realizing his full potential.

✓ He may develop mood disorders.

A natural outgrowth of child or youth molestation is anger. Self-directed anger can develop into depression. Sexual abuse also may prompt a neurochemical imbalance that triggers depression. Mood disturbances can affect sleep and eating patterns. Many people with eating disorders have reported childhood sexual assault as well.

✓ He may show rage and anger.

These feelings are common in children who feel frustrated, used, and invisible. Combined with their distorted thinking, they can misread another person's good intentions and lash out, believing they've been slighted. As adults, they may have issues with anger and can even become abusive themselves.

✓ His chances of getting help are slim.

Children and youth who are not supported by therapeutic intervention are at risk to later develop Posttraumatic Stress Disorder, also referred to as Post-traumatic Stress Syndrome, a cluster of characteristics that reflect severe anxiety. Anxiety can affect how people, learn, play, and cope with life stresses.

Any abnormal arousal sex patterns introduced during his sexual abuse are not redirected or curbed.

Negative sexual arousal habits may continue to be reinforced and can later lead to high-risk behavior or sexual attraction to children as well.

THE IMPORTANCE OF LISTENING TO YOUR CHILD

Even children who experience mild forms of molestation for short periods can develop problems when they're not believed or given enough support. Parents who don't address their child's molestation are demonstrating negligence, another type of child abuse.

Children and youth report molestation because they know they are in a situation they can't handle on their own. Parents may feel repulsion when they learn of a disclosure, emotionally withdrawing out of guilt or embarrassment or simply because they are overwhelmed. Assume your parental responsibilities by supporting your child. Sexual abuse is a burden he must not carry alone.

Chapter Four discusses other effects of child sexual abuse, along with revealing new research that validates a sexually abused child's behaviors.

Physical and Emotional Signs of Child and Youth Sexual Abuse

Even when your child hasn't disclosed anything, you may still wonder if she has been molested. If your suspicions are confirmed, investigators will want to know if she exhibits any signs that reflect her experience. In addition, when children develop physical and emotional problems as a result of their sexual abuse, they need immediate therapeutic intervention, so it's important to understand sexual abuse indicators.

A good way to recognize any fallout from sexual abuse is to understand normal sexual development in children. In addition to other signs, departure from age-appropriate sexual behavior is one that should raise red flags. The norms in the following reality check can help to give you a clearer picture of sexual development. They are not rigid; rather, they are guidelines subject to circumstances and individual children.

Reality Check 6: Sexual Development in Children

✓ Before birth: Sexual development in humans begins in the womb. Male fetuses show reflex erections weeks before birth. It is believed that female fetuses have corresponding clitoral arousal and spontaneous vaginal lubrication.

✓ Infancy: Infant penis and clitoral erections soon after birth are normal, especially during nursing. Arousal is a reflex reaction to the pleasant nursing sensation. Infants are unaware of these reflexes. As with many other child sexual behaviors, it is how parents react that may have the greatest effect on children.

✓ Under one year: As their motor skills develop, children begin exploring their genitals and receive pleasure from touching themselves. Orgasms have been observed in children under the age of one.

✓ By age two: Boys and girls know they are different from the other sex by comparing their bodies. They express natural curiosity and will grasp the concept of public and private questions and behavior in a few more years.

✓ Ages two to five: Children are interested in their own as well as others' genitals. They'll compare and explore through imitative games such as "playing doctor and nurse" or "mommy and daddy." William H. Masters and Virginia Johnson's studies on human sexuality in the 1970s indicate that during these play activities, they look, touch, and sometimes attempt to insert objects into body openings.

Children living in crowded housing may observe adults having sex and mimic their behavior. They don't understand what it means.

Children often ask questions about where babies come from and will literally believe (if told) that storks do bring them.

Small children find bathroom humor very funny. They will get a kick out of words like *butt*, *wiener*, *boobs*, and *pee*.

✓ By age five, most children are in school and participating in more structured activities. They often become more modest, but the jokes continue, even when they don't fully understood them.

✓ By the time kids are six and seven, they're clearer in their understanding about the physical differences between the sexes, and their sense of modesty becomes stronger. Natural curiosity is expressed through game playing again, with the same or opposite sex. Sex play between two boys or two girls is in no way an indication of sexual preference. These activities are normal and mutual. Abuse occurs when one child coerces another child using force or threats.

✓ By ages seven and eight, children are aware of what is considered sexy within a society. These messages are conveyed through the media, computer games, and the behaviors of older people.

Experimentation goes underground as children become more aware of social rules. They are still interested in sexual stimulation. Mutual masturbation with someone of the same sex is not unusual because the opposite sex may seem foreign or scary. Experimenting with same-sex friends is less intimidating.

✓ As early as age nine or ten, some girls begin their periods, and boys may have nocturnal emissions ("wet dreams"). Children may feel confused by these experiences and their growing sexuality. In spite of the openness in our society, children can be surprisingly naive. Many times, they are given the wrong information by other children and sometimes by their own parents. Unless they receive correct information, they may carry myths about human sexuality into adulthood.

Some parents of sexually abused children have incorrectly assumed their child "knew what she was getting into" or was aware of other important information such as birth control. Many have voiced amazement when they learned otherwise.

✓ During adolescence (when secondary sex organs develop: pubic hair and other body hair, breasts, testicle growth, and so forth), children practice sexual behaviors through dating, in groups, or alone. They mimic the dress and behaviors of people who appear to be independent. Separation from parents by way of establishing their own identity is an important stage in their development.

ACUTE STRESS AND POSTTRAUMATIC STRESS SYNDROME

Children often develop physical and psychological problems as a result of their sexual abuse. Their problems vary depending on such factors as the child's age and the type, intensity, and duration of her assault, as well as therapeutic support.

An example of less severe sexual assault is an adult's exposing himself to a group of children on their way to school. The experience could traumatize any of them; they may experience nightmares and later become anxious about walking in that neighborhood. When these anxiety symptoms last from two days to one month, they're called *acute stress*.

Sexual assault such as rape can have a more severe impact on children. As a result, they can develop a number of serious problems that include depression, self-mutilation, or drug addiction.

If symptoms following a sexual assault last longer than one month children can develop Posttraumatic Stress Syndrome/Disorder (PTSD). In either case, intervention is needed. Children need to

> ## Acute Stress
>
> Acute stress occurs when children are exposed to a traumatic experience and then develop anxiety and worry. The condition lasts at least two days but generally not more than one month and includes feeling numb and detached, reexperiencing the trauma through flashbacks or nightmares, avoiding experiences that are associated with the trauma, and feeling significant anxiety that interferes with normal functioning.

talk, write, or express their anxiety in some way with their counselors or caregivers.

Personal and physical histories also have a lot to do with the severity of symptoms and how children recover from sexual abuse. (Keep in mind that some children do not develop problems, especially those who receive immediate help.) Children have a better chance of recovery when they get help—the sooner, the better.

THE PHYSICAL CONDITION BEHIND ACUTE AND POSTTRAUMATIC STRESS DISORDERS

All human beings respond to terrifying situations in pretty much the same way. When we become frightened, an automatic alarm sounds within our brains and bodies, triggering a freezing or fight-or-flight response. Physical and emotional trauma causes this survival response. Child sexual abuse is one trauma example. (There are many, and they include car accidents, natural disasters, chronic illness, and other forms of abuse.)

When we experience trauma, a disruption can take place in our normal neurological functioning as a surge in survival hormones floods the brain. As a result, our neural chemicals may become out

Jack's Story

Jack's mother used drugs during her pregnancy, and when he was born, his motor skills were somewhat delayed. Later, his ability to learn was delayed as well. At age seven, while participating in an after-care program at school, Jack's sweet and eager-to-please disposition was spotted by a day care worker, who began to take Jack behind the stage curtain and fondle him.

Jack began to call his caregiver his "special" friend. His inquisitive mother asked him why this person was so special, and Jack explained that he received prizes for being loved. His mom followed up on her intuition, and a sexual abuse investigation was initiated.

Instead of expressing relief, Jack cried when his "friend" left school and reported he was scared about sending the man away. Jack's counselor and mother stressed to Jack that he had done nothing wrong, but because of his disability, Jack's capacity to grasp the situation was impaired.

Eventually Jack understood the concept of "good touch/bad touch" as well as ways to protect himself from further abuse. Some time later, he stated that he knew his teacher had done a "bad" thing, but it had taken a while for him to get to that realization.

of balance, and even our brain structure can change (see the Additional Information section for more on disruption of normal brain function). These changes can create anxious body and mind conditions. The chronic or ongoing conditions can later lead children to try to control them through anxiety calming or avoidance behaviors that over time become habits. Posttraumatic Stress Disorder/

Posttraumatic Stress Disorder/Syndrome

The name *Posttraumatic Stress Disorder* first appeared in the 1980s, but it has a long history. It had previously been known as combat fatigue and in the nineteenth century was referred to as DaCosta's syndrome.

In both acute and posttraumatic stress, a child has experienced, witnessed, or been confronted with actual or threatened death or injury or a threat to her or another's body. Her response is intensely fearful and elicits feelings of helplessness and horror.

Posttraumatic stress symptoms are similar to acute stress. Trauma is persistently reexperienced through images, thoughts, or perceptions. Children will avoid triggers that remind them of their trauma and experience-numbing reactions, and they can be excessively anxious or aroused. If these conditions go unattended, it can eventually affect the child's developing beliefs and worldview.

Syndrome and Acute Stress Disorder are the diagnosis labels that identify these behaviors or habits.

Here is the way that sexual abuse sets up a reaction that ends with PTSD:

Sexual abuse ⟶ physical and emotional trauma.

Trauma ⟶ fear and terror.

Fear and terror ⟶ survival response.

Survival response ⟶ brain and body reaction.

Brain and body reaction ⟶ anxiety.

Anxiety ⟶ coping behaviors. Coping behaviors are repeated and become habits, or PTSD.

Symbolic or literal associations to the original trauma can trigger the survival response again and lead children to believe they are still experiencing their trauma.

ASSOCIATION TRIGGERS
PROMPT ANXIOUS RESPONSES

Sexual abuse trauma can cause symptoms listed in Reality Check 7. These symptoms reflect how children and youth consciously or unconsciously cope with their anxiety. They can become more obvious when anxiety is triggered by reminders of past sexual abuse. Children are seldom aware of these triggers, and their reactions seem to come from out of nowhere.

Even when they are no longer abused, children can be triggered into a survival/anxious reaction, including reexperiencing their trauma. Sometimes they experience flashbacks—internal images that make it seem as if their abuse is still happening. Consequently, children need to be reassured that they're safe in spite of the fact that their brains and bodies are responding as though they're still in danger. Here are some trigger examples:

- Loud noises

- Discussion about their sexual abuse

- Dressing or undressing

- Certain music, sounds, smells, or textures

- Stress

- Certain anniversaries, such as deaths, birthdays, and sexual assault

- Sexual contact

- Bathing

- Physical examinations

- Reminders of their perpetrator

- Certain hours of the day, such as bedtime

- Exposure to weapons

- Television programs or video games

- Nightmares

- Certain adult behaviors such as drinking, arguing, or rejection

- Periods of calm

- Certain rituals, such as kneeling, lighting candles, or locking doors

- Being held down

Reality Check 7: Sexual Abuse Signs and Symptoms

✓ Shows excessive aggression toward animals

✓ Displays seemingly irrational fear or dislike for another person

✓ Engages in aggressive, disruptive behavior (please see the Additional Information section in the back of the book)

✓ Runs away

✓ Fails school

✓ Displays antisocial behavior such as stealing, hurting others, or setting fires

✓ Shows mood disorders: depression, mania, anxiety, hypersensitivity

✓ Has unexplained fears about undressing at school, following normal routines, or worrying about a sibling's whereabouts

✓ Obsessively washes hands or adopts other compulsive routines

✓ Locks doors and takes extreme safety precautions

✓ Has difficulty concentrating and learning; daydreams

✓ Develops memory problems or cannot remember blocks of time (please see the Additional Information section in the back of the book)

✓ Displays body tension

✓ Becomes impulsive

✓ Is easily startled (called exaggerated startle response)

✓ Becomes hypervigilant about personal space or safety

✓ Clings to adults or other caregivers

✓ Attempts or threatens suicide

✓ Changes in usual behaviors; withdrawing from activities, sudden shyness, or excessive crying

✓ Appetite disturbance: gorging, gagging, throwing up, no appetite

✓ Nightmares, disturbed sleep patterns

✓ Regression in behavior: sucking the thumb, bed-wetting, baby talk, tantrums, and so forth

✓ Excessive masturbation

✓ Panic

✓ Self-mutilation: cutting self, excessive tattoos and body piercing

✓ Complaints of pain while urinating or having bowel movements

✓ Pregnancy

✓ Torn or stained nightgowns, pajamas, or underwear

✓ Vaginal or rectal bleeding, pain, itching, swollen genitals, vaginal discharge, unusual genital odor, or sexually transmitted diseases such as hepatitis B or C

✓ Unusual interest in or knowledge of sexual matters: Reenacting the sexual abuse with toys, animals, other children, or adults and disclosing sophisticated information about human sexuality

✓ Your child has frequent colds or other health problems. (Trauma affects the immune system.) Sexually abused children may develop stomach pains, headaches, other aches, or unexplained rashes.

✓ Your child is engaging in drug or alcohol experimentation.

Many of the indicators just listed fall into the categories of acute and posttraumatic stress. Any one of these behaviors does not necessarily confirm sexual molestation, but pay special attention if the symptom is relatively new or dramatic and if your child is obsessive about it. Medical problems such as sexually transmitted diseases or swollen or bleeding genitals indicate sexual abuse as well. And remember that children molested over a long period may not appear different in their behavior.

SCOTT'S BEHAVIOR AFTER THE ABUSE

Scott had withdrawn from participating in his camping club, something he previously enjoyed, and he had become moody and irritable. His parents noticed these changes, and Scott's dad took time to casually question his son when they painted their boat.

Scott was affected by the abuse, and his anxiety came to light during his early discussions with his father. Had his parents not followed up on Scott's comments, the boy's fears may have escalated. His anxiety about being homosexual might never have been addressed, and he may have stopped communicating with his parents.

Reenactment Signs

Following a molestation, a child may show behaviors that appear to be deliberately seductive. These behaviors have been reinforced by her perpetrator. Because they were encouraged, younger children in particular are confused when other adults become judgmental or rejecting. For example, if a teacher doesn't understand sexual abuse, she could easily inflict further psychological harm by her reaction.

Here are a few signs to watch for in your child:

- Locks her door when a friend comes to play

- Demonstrates angry, demanding behavior around other children

- Persuades another child to engage in "sexy" dressing or spends a good deal of time engaging in sexually provocative activities

- Mimics adult sexual behaviors with adults and other children

---

Under the same circumstances, other parents may have been embarrassed or cut their children off by never addressing the issue or helping to relieve their anxiety. Consequently, they contribute to the problem.

STRIKING A BALANCE

You need to strike a balance between overreacting and overlooking signs of sexual abuse. If you suspect your child has been molested, speak to her in a gentle, nonthreatening way, much like Scott's dad

Suicide Warning Signs

Sexual abuse has been named as one factor behind suicide or attempted suicide. The National Institute of Mental Health reports that suicide is now the leading cause of death in ten to fourteen year olds. A startling 21 percent of high school students report they contemplated suicide within the past year, and 8 percent have made suicide attempts. Here are some signals that may indicate your child is contemplating suicide:

- Your child expresses worry, hopelessness, moroseness, irritability, sorrow, and/or euphoria for at least a week.

- Your child makes statements such as "If I were gone, it would be easier on everyone," or "I wish I could sleep and never wake up," or "Life isn't worth living."

- Your child describes a suicide plan and her funeral.

- Your child is psychologically vulnerable as a result of a disappointment, breakup, punishment, or shame.

- You notice your child has lost interest in her usual activities and has let her appearance decline.

- Your child takes excessive risks that include using addictive substances, engaging in unprotected sex, or driving recklessly.

- Your child has attempted suicide in the past.

- Your child gives away prized possessions.

did. Demonstrate your concern and support through your words and actions. Again, make it clear to your child that she did nothing wrong and everything right in letting you know. Let her know that you are keeping communication open. If there is anything else she wants to say, you are there to listen.

When investigators are brought into the picture, let them know when you first noticed the changes in your child. The information will help with their investigation.

As time goes by, refer back to the list in Reality Check 7. It can serve as a marker: as your child is making progress and moving nearer to recovery, you'll recognize that her symptoms surface less often and seem less severe.

Chapter Five introduces you to the professional helpers and describes their roles in the investigation, prosecution, and treatment of child sexual abuse.

Your Professional Support Team

Before reporting their child's disclosure, most parents haven't had much contact with police officers, child welfare workers, or prosecuting attorneys. This was true for Janet and Bill. They were understandably concerned about investigation procedures and wanted to protect Scott as much as possible. They also were wary of meeting strangers and exposing their son to embarrassing questions.

These worries are normal. Understanding the professionals with whom they would work helped to lessen their anxiety. A number of individuals and their respective agencies were involved with investigating the sexual abuse report, prosecuting the case, and counseling Scott and his family:

Paul Abrams, a detective with the Sexual Crimes Unit of the County Sheriff's Department

Fred Hedges, a child protection services investigator in the Sexual Abuse Unit, Department of Children and Families, provided through local government

Sally Johnson, case coordinator for the Child Protection Team, a child protection consulting agency attached to the community hospital

Jon Devlin, M.D., pediatrician and child abuse examiner, a contracted physician with the Child Protection Team, attached
to the community hospital

Brenda Hunter, J.D., prosecuting attorney

Philip Andrews, L.M.F.T., Licensed Marriage and Family
Therapist, contracted with the county sexual abuse treatment
center

Although members of support teams may have different titles
and varying jobs, the following descriptions are pretty universal:

• Detective Abrams was assigned to investigate the report
phoned in by the hot line coordinator after Janet's call. In the
Thompsons' community, the County Sheriff's Department takes the
initial call. In other communities, it may be the Department of
Children and Families. Because every jurisdiction is different, the
police representative may or may not have special training in handling sexual assault in children. It was fortunate that in this case,
Detective Abrams was working with a sexual crimes unit and up to
date on the best practice with these types of cases.

• Fred Hedges is a social worker in the sexual crimes unit of his
district's Department of Children and Families. Every community
has a child protection agency monitoring the protection of its children. Depending on where you live, children's service agencies usually fall under the umbrella of state or local governments.

Fred is a child abuse investigations worker who will accompany
Detective Abrams when they meet with Scott for the first interview.
If Fred thinks a child is in immediate danger, he will make a quick
assessment and after consultation with a supervisor temporarily
remove him from his environment. Fred will be involved because
Mr. Webster was considered to be in a caretaker position. A person
with the child protective services is involved when the molester is
either a custodial person or extended family member.

• Sally Johnson is a social worker with the Child Protection Team, a consulting agency contracted to work with both law enforcement and human service agencies. (In other parts of the country, her agency is referred to as the Sexual Assault Team, Advocacy Center, or Children's Crisis Unit.) Sally will assist Detective Abrams and Fred Hedges by providing her agency's special interviewing room for the formal interview, interviewing Scott, and if necessary scheduling Scott's medical examination. She will also coordinate any victim advocacy for his family and make the referral to the therapist, Philip Andrews.

Sally's specialized training in interviewing abused children will be used when she interviews Scott. In her role, she serves as a liaison between the various agencies. The Child Protection Team, Sally's agency, has only the authority delegated to it by the other agencies.

• Dr. Jon Devlin is a pediatrician who contracts with the Child Protection Team to examine children for signs of physical trauma due to physical or sexual abuse. In some communities, a county health department may oversee the examinations. In other locations, a doctor may be on staff with a rape treatment agency. In emergency situations, children may be seen by emergency room doctors.

• Brenda Hunter is an assistant prosecuting attorney who prosecutes criminal cases on behalf of the state. She assesses the evidence brought to her by the investigation team to see if prosecution is justified. She will review their information along with the interview videotape in preparing the criminal charges against the alleged sex offender. She will more than likely be present and argue the case throughout the court process. Prosecuting attorneys working on behalf of their jurisdiction have other titles, such as magistrate, district attorney, or county or city attorney. In some locations, attorneys are assigned to work on only child sexual abuse cases.

• Philip Andrews is a licensed mental health professional who contracts with the Child Protection Team to work with abused children and their families. Phil received special training in the treatment of physically and sexually abused kids beyond his master's degree in counseling. In other locations, children see private or community mental health therapists. Mental health costs can be provided free through victim advocacy programs, on a sliding-scale basis, through personal insurance programs, or through first-party payment (meaning that parents pay the costs).

Scott would interact with at least five of these people and all six if he is examined by Dr. Devlin. At some point, if recommended by Phil, he may be referred for a medication evaluation to a child psychiatrist or nurse practitioner. The services available to the Thompson family are comprehensive. In some communities, parents communicate only through the police departments or work most of the time with the child welfare office. Other communities don't have a child protection team. And sometimes agencies rely on parents to coordinate their own services.

If you live in an area where there are no specialized professional services, you can access through the Internet national child welfare associations that offer information that may answer your questions. Some include the National Center for Missing and Exploited Children (www.missingkids.com), Children's Defense Fund (www.childrensdefense.org), and The Child Welfare League of America (www.cwla.org).

Even if services in your area are not what you'd hoped would be available, you and your family can still benefit from their assistance. Understanding how to work most effectively with your support team is described in the following chapter.

Victim Advocacy

Victim advocacy has progressed a long way in recent years. If legal action is taken in criminal cases, families are usually eligible to receive victim crime compensation to support them on their way to recovery. There are other services as well—for example:

- Victim advocates, who prepare and accompany victims to court

- Rapid-response social workers, who work in schools

- Case coordinators, who help facilitate in-home services and access other resources, such as transportation to appointments

- Advocates for developmentally challenged or disabled victims, who bridge gaps between services

- Victim advocate translators, who assist in translating languages or otherwise providing culturally appropriate interviews and communication

- Prevention advocates, who teach children about "good touch" and "bad touch" and speak to youth about rape prevention

6

The Formal/Forensic Interview

Helping Investigators Work Effectively with Your Child

Whether you work with just one or a team of professionals, investigators agree that parents need to be informed. Use the following helpful reminders as you prepare your child for her formal, sometimes referred to as forensic, interview, which occurs after authorities have completed their initial meeting with your child:

• Resist going over the details of her disclosure unless your child brings it up. Even then, don't try to interpret her information, and keep your remarks simple and vague. You may say something like, "I understand" or "I see."

• Keep adult conversations regarding the abuse away from your child. Phone calls and any other conversations at a store or around relatives can be overhead. Be careful about what you say in front of your other children as well.

• Don't use sophisticated legal terms around your child. And resist correcting her references to her genitals if she has always referred to them in simple terms such as *pee-pee* or *poopie*.

• Be reasonable with regard to demands about prosecuting the alleged perpetrator. Prosecutors report that they've heard every kind of response from parents. Sometimes families adopt a self-protective attitude or demand the electric chair.

OTHER CONSIDERATIONS

After reporting the sexual abuse to the hot line, you may be called by the investigator to schedule a formal interview after his initial meeting with your child. Be sure to suggest scheduling times that stack the cards in your child's direction, so that she is in the best possible frame of mind. A tired or hungry child doesn't interview well. And let the investigator know if your child is particularly fearful of anything such as uniformed people or certain environments. This is also a good time to ask other questions, such as the estimated length of the interview and whether more interviews will be needed, who will take part in the interview, how it will be conducted, and if your child will be examined by a physician immediately following the formal interview.

Your state may have a limit on the number of times a child can be interviewed during the investigation process. Limiting the number of interviews helps to maintain a friendly association with the investigators and cooperation from your child. A single videotaped or audiotaped interview, when conducted properly, offers the advantages of reducing the number of times your child has to tell her story.

You will be interviewed about the allegations separately from your child, usually as part of the interview process. At this time, you will be asked about the disclosure and possible behavior changes in your child. You will also be asked if you believe the allegations.

This is a good time to ask your own questions and record the answers you receive for future reference. Be sure to jot down the names and telephone numbers of the professionals working with your child, although they will give you their business cards. Remember to record all your meetings, and at the end of each, ask about the next step, who will be involved, and a general time line for getting back to you with any information. This information will help keep you organized and help you recall information later when you're under less emotional stress.

Before the formal interview, you can help your child feel comfortable by letting her know she is going someplace to talk to a helper about what happened. Sometimes children become more frightened when they learn they'll be talking to a stranger, so gently introduce the topic in a calm, casual manner. Reassure her that the people she'll be speaking with don't judge or gossip. It may be reassuring for her to bring along a favorite blanket or toy. Older children may want to wear a favorite piece of jewelry or carry a "lucky" stone. Let her know that you will be sitting nearby but won't be able to hear her conversation. If your child expresses worry or asks questions, try to respond to her concerns before the interview. Remember that most people feel anxious in new settings and speaking to strangers. Continue to assure your younger child that being videotaped does not mean that it will be played on televisions in other people's homes.

Depending on their age and emotional development, children will behave differently during their interview. The following reality check shares other factors as well about the interview.

Reality Check 8: Establishing Reasonable Expectations with Your Child

✓ Preverbal children are difficult to interview and many times cannot be interviewed at all. Verbal communication usually becomes possible with children sometime between the ages of two and three.

✓ Children with developmental disabilities may need additional support with interviewers who understand their needs.

✓ Children ages two to four have difficulty understanding time frames and other concepts, though their language may indicate otherwise.

✓ Preschoolers can usually follow a single thought at a time.

✓ Young children often tire of talking about what happened and become distracted quickly.

✓ Many children become anxious when they discuss their abuse. They may become agitated, need to check on their parents, or change the subject.

✓ Depending on how they're asked, children may give different answers to the same question.

✓ Although much of their play focuses on pretend, preschoolers can usually distinguish between fantasy and fact.

✓ Preschoolers can remember an isolated incident more vividly when it is associated with something memorable—for example, a certain time of day such as bedtime or play time, a television program, a holiday, or a season.

✓ Most children are embarrassed when they talk about their abuse and seldom have the correct words to describe it. It's not that they won't discuss it; they just don't know how.

✓ Younger children may ramble when talking about their experience and include extraneous information.

✓ Young children in general often think adults can tell when they are lying.

✓ After age six, children better understand the interview process.

THE INTERVIEW

It is likely that you will not be included when your child is interviewed. Simply by their presence, parents can influence their kids. And it can be easier at times for children to talk to a stranger without a parent in the room.

Preserving the interview on videotape gives the prosecutor valuable information and helps her assess your child's effectiveness as a witness. Videotaping allows the prosecutor to review the material more than once and records a child's body language as well. In effect, it is your child's statement.

Understand that sometimes children don't provide adequate information in the formal interview. They can become frustrated if they've already disclosed, thinking they are not being believed. As a result, they may begin to hold back or make up "facts" or even change their answers. If they've been told by the alleged perpetrator not to tell anyone what happened, they may think the offender may magically know about the disclosure. Other times, kids just feel uncomfortable and embarrassed.

Sally Johnson, the case coordinator from the Child Protection Team, interviewed Scott Thompson. When Scott and his parents arrived at the Child Protection Team interview site, she asked the family if they wanted to look around. She took them on a brief tour, pausing to describe the interview room, two-way mirror, and videotaping equipment and introduce those who would be observing the interview on the other side of the two-way mirror. (Fred Hedges, the child protection services investigator, and Detective Abrams would be observing.)

She took time prior to the interview to obtain a thorough physical and social history about Scott from his parents. A comprehensive background search through Detective Abrams's computer information system had already been completed, so the support team had as much information as possible. After she had completed verifying Scott's history with Bill and Janet, they waited in the lounge while Sally guided Scott through the interview.

Sally took time to help Scott feel comfortable. She carefully chose her words, not wishing to be leading with her questions. And she was calm and patient, taking pains not to rush Scott through the interview. (If children want to stop the process, their wishes are honored.)

After the interview, Sally told Scott that she needed to speak with his parents. Handing him her business card, she encouraged him to phone her with any questions. Speaking again only with Scott's parents, the support team shared information disclosed in the interview and gave their recommendations. Among other things, Sally recommended that the entire family begin counseling, and she gave them Phil Andrews's business card as well as names of other therapists. She gave them a few brochures on her agency and other helpful pieces of advice, such as victim advocacy services. She further explained that the tape and report would be reviewed with Brenda, the prosecuting attorney. She would be getting back to the Thompsons as soon as possible, giving them an approximate time line. Detective Abrams and Fred Hedges were present to discuss further procedures and share any time lines as well.

When Janet and Bill asked if Scott needed to be examined by a pediatrician, Sally said that under the circumstances, it wasn't necessary. Nothing other than fondling had been reported, she said, and for now, they wanted Scott's experience to be as least intrusive as possible.

Driving home, Janet and Bill were careful not to ask Scott to describe the interview. Kids will usually initiate discussion. They did, however, check in with Scott by asking him if he was okay, using a scale from one to ten, with ten being the most okay. Scott stated he was about a six. The Thompsons were careful to observe Scott's behavior throughout the evening.

THE PHYSICAL EXAMINATION

The forensic physical examination occurs when children have disclosed sexual assault or if the forensic interview indicates a strong likelihood of molestation. In some states, parental permission is not needed for an exam to occur with adolescents, but permission forms are signed anyway to have a record that parents know about the procedure. (It's helpful to remember that examinations are not frivolously administered and that about 4 percent of children determined to be sexually molested show physical signs through their examinations.)

Examinations are conducted at child advocacy or child protection centers by specially trained pediatricians with facilities designed particularly for children and adolescents. Kids are asked whom they would like to have with them during the exam. Doctors spend most of their time gathering information, comparing it with the formal interview, and helping the child to feel comfortable. The examination itself takes about ten minutes, and a case coordinator is usually present. Prepubescent children are examined differently than postpubescent youth are.

Prepubescent Children

After taking a medical history and spending time getting to know the child, the doctor does an external exam. Because children often report that the most traumatic part of the exam was taking blood, many physicians will have it drawn later (if blood tests are even necessary). Internal examinations are rarely done, and the speculum is not used. If an internal examination is needed, it proceeds with the child under sedation. If there is strong suspicion of the presence of sexually transmitted diseases (STDs), the doctor will have her tested. However, STDs seldom occur in children, and their symptoms are fairly obvious.

At the end of the examination, doctors are careful to reassure their young patients they did nothing wrong and that sexual abuse does not mark them as damaged.

Adolescent Youth

After spending time taking a thorough medical history, the physician will proceed with an external exam. If there is sufficient reason, the doctor will proceed with an internal examination. A documentation protocol follows for gathering evidence such as sperm or pubic hair. Because STD symptoms are more subtle for adolescent youth, tests are ordered more often than they are for children. Positive tests, which occur with 5 to 7 percent of adolescents, don't always signify sexual assault because some teenagers are sexually active. And again, blood may not be drawn until later.

DNA testing is administered to gather trace evidence if there is suspicion of impregnation or if the case is going to court. Swabbing the mouth is the newest way to proceed as opposed to taking blood. Law enforcement labs generally handle DNA tests.

At the end of the exam, physicians spend time reassuring their young patients.

The Test Results

There are different time lines for getting back test results. Most of the time, HIV and other STD test results can be accessed within forty-eight hours. DNA test results usually take around ten days.

Depending on where you live, the test results may be shared only with your adolescent. Doctor-patient confidentiality is important and stringent, yet cases going to court sometimes force health conditions such as an STD to come to the attention of other helping professionals.

Follow-up interviews are arranged after the physical examination so that further needs can be determined and children and youth experience continuity of care.

AFTER THE INTERVIEW

After the interview and medical examination, your child may be unusually quiet or anxious. Allow her to express her feelings. A stop for a hamburger, a quiet walk, or a story can be calming. Continue to reassure her that she was brave to tell the truth. Be careful not

Telemedicine

Telemedicine networks provide forensic services to areas of the country where resources are difficult to access. This approach allows the performance of child sexual abuse assessments through information and computer technologies between "hub" sites and "remote" sites. Hub sites are located at medical facilities with a wide range of medical and multidisciplinary professional staff. Remote sites are smaller medical facilities in remote areas with limited access to comprehensive care. The equipment used enables hubs to provide direction and consultation while observing remote interviews and examinations. This approach allows the child abuse expert to become the examiner of record and appropriately guide colleagues in the remote area through proper examination and interview protocol.

to interrogate her. Yet asking simple questions is okay. Scott's folks chose to use a "feeling scale" to gain information, but it's just as easy to ask, "Do you feel sad, mad, or glad?"

Children may feel relief after their interview. They may be reenergized or extra tired. Let your child know that her formal interview did not mean that she would never speak to the investigators again or that the case ends there. The reality is that your child may be interviewed again, give a deposition, or appear as a witness.

There is also a possibility that the case is dropped at this point for lack of sufficient evidence. Be prepared to feel disappointed if this should happen. It's okay to share your disappointment with your child, but be careful not to overreact. In addition, you need to let your child know that what she did was still right, that she did nothing wrong, and that together you will seek support through counseling.

If the process does not go further than the formal interview, you have the option to pursue other avenues with the advice of an attorney, such as taking civil action.

WHAT PARENTS SAY

During the investigation process, parents can experience a full range of emotions, and more than a few have later regretted their behavior. Caregivers may express regret when they've had an opportunity to reflect on their actions following their children's disclosures. Here are a few of their remarks:

> "I was so caught up in my own confusion and anger that I didn't realize how badly my child needed my support. After her interview, I drilled her about everything that was said. I didn't realize that my behavior made her feel personally responsible for sending her molester to jail."

> "We wish we had told our son that the presence of a police officer didn't mean he'd done anything wrong. We didn't let him know that investigators are there to help."

> "I'm sorry I told my daughter it would be her fault if the babysitter didn't get punished after she'd forgotten to tell the investigators about his threats to keep things quiet."

> "When my child described her abuse, I corrected her until her story was clearer. But when she was interviewed, she used *my* words, and the case was dropped because the investigators believed she'd been coached."

TAKE A DEEP BREATH,
BUT DON'T FORGET TO EXHALE

The investigation stage can be anxiety provoking because no one can give you a direct answer about the direction the case will go until the prosecutor's office makes its decision.

If you feel frustrated, share your feelings with other understanding adults, your spouse, your investigation team, friends, or a therapist. But remind yourself to keep your emotions in check around your child.

Once you've gotten through the formal interview congratulate yourself, your partner, and your child. You've completed the second stage of your journey. Then take a deep breath and prepare yourself for the potentially slow judicial process. The next chapter explains delays you may encounter and provides helpful suggestions on how to cope when the legal process seems to crawl.

The Judicial Process
Why It Takes a While

After your call to the hot line, you and your child will likely become involved in the investigation and prosecution process, as well as counseling. Your child's sexual abuse may become the central issue in your life. And while regular life continues, pressures have been added to it.

This extra pressure can put a strain on your family, so eagerly anticipating an end to the judicial process is normal. If it moves slowly, you can expect to feel irritation and frustration.

Our expectations about law and order can be somewhat unrealistic because we may use television as a reality check. On television shows, the crime occurs, the police solve the case, the alleged perpetrator goes to trial and is found guilty, and the victim and his family return to normal life, all within thirty to sixty minutes. Although all of us recognize on a conscious level that things don't happen that way, we may be unconsciously affected by the resolution speed in these programs.

In real cases, steps can proceed at a frustratingly slow pace. The legal system requires a prescribed course of action, and delays are normal. For example, Bill and Janet Thompson heard nothing for several days after Scott's interview. When they phoned Sally at the Child Protection Team, they were reminded that all the children in Scott's camping club needed to be interviewed before the case could proceed.

When Janet phoned Detective Abrams with a question, she was put on hold for several minutes. After the operator returned, she was given his voice message indicating he was on vacation. When Janet attempted to reach his supervisor, the man was unable to return her message for a few days. Then she was told only that the detectives were working on the case to the best of their ability.

Janet felt that she had received a stock answer from a stranger who was unfamiliar with their situation. And she and Bill felt powerless about prompting the wheels of justice to move faster. Their conversations with each other ran along the lines of those of the other parents. Didn't anybody care what happened to their son and the other boys?

Bill was not surprised when he came home the following evening and found Janet angrily typing a letter to the police chief complaining that she and her husband were fed up with the way they'd been treated and exhausted by the demands from the police department. She wanted to know why so much effort was made to protect the rights of the alleged offender.

GETTING A HANDLE ON FRUSTRATION THROUGH COUNSELING

The Thompsons had been wise to begin their counseling with Phil Andrews soon after the formal interview. Phil helped them recognize they didn't have a lot of control over the situation. With his guidance, they began concentrating on the things they could control. When they took Phil's advice and started to work on their feelings and Scott's trauma recovery, their focus changed and their frustration diminished.

During one of their first family sessions, Phil explained that because things happen slowly, it doesn't mean that their support team isn't doing its job or that no one cares. If everything were rushed, he said, confusion and mistakes could result. Carefulness can be misinterpreted as laziness. If all the facts aren't gathered before charges are filed, the case may not have enough substantial evidence to convince the prosecutor's office that they are justified.

Phil noted that once Scott and the other boys were determined to be safe, there was no need to rush the investigation. Better coordination among the support agencies was more likely. With time on their side, the team members were able to meet and strategize their next steps in the process.

HOW CASES ARE HANDLED

States vary with regard to prosecuting sex offenders. And the administrative attitude toward child sexual assault can make a difference. In some cases, prosecutors are more proactive and will request additional witness statements. Other prosecutors leave it totally up to investigators to gather and prepare the information. Only then do the prosecutors make a determination.

Prosecuting alleged sex offenders can take time. Prosecutors' offices are historically busy, and proceeding in frivolous cases (those in which there is no chance of obtaining conviction) waste valuable time. In addition, on rare occasions, investigators, by virtue of the fact they too are extremely busy, may make a mistake in the investigation, to the point of making a conviction unlikely.

At times, the period between making the hot line phone call and arrest is short. If a child is determined to be in immediate danger and there is probable cause to suspect the alleged perpetrator, a warrant for his arrest can be obtained if he has not fled. It's simply a matter of obtaining a warrant and making the arrest. (There can be understandable delays when a defendant deliberately makes himself scarce.)

MORE ABOUT THE WAIT

The period between the arrest and final outcome of your child's case can seem to drag on forever. Sadly, many families put their lives on hold during this time, forgetting that it is the legal system's responsibility to deal with the alleged molester.

Although laws have become more conservative and alleged perpetrators are not bonded out of jail as easily as in the past, it can be difficult to understand why an alleged perpetrator who was arrested in the morning may be bonded out and mowing his lawn in the afternoon.

Even people who have blatantly broken sexual taboos with children have the same legal rights as you, and those rights must be protected so that innocent people are protected. The system isn't perfect, but in the end it usually works.

Other aspects of the legal proceedings may be confusing. For instance, sentencing guidelines differ from state to state and can depend on the nature of the abuse and alleged perpetrator's criminal record. Some sentences have become standardized, so that there is a degree of continuity about what happens when a person is convicted of a particular offense. This limits the judge's discretion when imposing what she or he feels to be an appropriate punishment.

It's not unusual for a trial to be held as long as several months after the arrest. Sometimes this delay works to your advantage because you can better prepare your child for appearing in court and establish a psychological distance between you and the alleged offender.

Keeping your eye on helping your child will help you experience less frustration if the legal process slows down. And don't allow your feelings to build to the extent that you boil over and deliver ultimatums, such as calling the local newspaper or TV station.

Making a weekly phone call to inquire about the status of your child's case is perfectly okay and may provide you with new information. Getting feedback can be reassuring and lessen your anxiety. Check-in calls also provide you with an opportunity to share other information, such as scheduling plans or even freshly remembered disclosure information.

Jurisdictions vary as to how much judicial consideration is given to caregiver input. In criminal cases such as Scott's, the state prosecutes the accused. How the case is prosecuted is totally out of the hands of the victim or his family. Under certain circumstances, however, the court may consider the wishes of the child and his family if the defendant wishes to plea-bargain his case. Let the prosecutor know as soon as possible if you wish to give input.

When a Case Does or Does Not Go to Trial

If a plea agreement is reached before the case goes to trial, your child will be spared having to give depositions and additional interviews and be readied for court testimony. But be prepared to hear that the defendant has received a lesser sentence that may include probation or community-based treatment.

If a case goes to trial, it will involve depositions given by your child and perhaps family members or other key witnesses, as well as possible court testimony and any other mandatory court procedures. The process may be lengthy and the experience potentially retraumatizing for your child. Yet, sometimes children feel empowered by appearing in court. Good preparation is the key in how you and your family handle the situation.

THE DEFENSE ATTORNEY'S ROLE

In some jurisdictions, defense attorneys get all of the *continuances*, or approved delays, they request. Continuances are considered and ultimately decided by the presiding judge. If judges feel that denying continuances will result in later appeals because the defense did not have adequate time for trial preparation, they will grant a continuance.

One judge related, "It's heartbreaking for a judge to come into a trial where witnesses are subpoenaed and assembled and the jurors are available, but one or the other legal team is not ready. Because we're dealing with lawyers with heavy case loads, we often grant a continuance. We have very little choice because there are serious rights and consequences involved. Often it's a question of resources. If we had more public defenders and prosecutors, court-connected counselors and evaluators, we could change things. Inadequate staffing, because of lack of funds, is the basic problem."

Defense attorneys may see delays to their advantage. One attorney remarked that "the three D's of defense are Dilly, Dally, and Delay." Defense attorneys feel that the longer a trial is delayed, the more weary the victim's family will become. They sometimes tell families that if they don't want to go through with depositions or repeated interviews, they can drop the case. This cannot happen if criminal court is involved because it is the *state's* case.

One prosecuting attorney says, "If people are putting a lot of pressure on the family to drop the case, I remind them to say that the decision is the state's, not the family's. Some prosecutors will even tell pressured parents to phone them in the presence of those applying the pressure and say 'I want the case dropped.' Our reply gets people off their backs." (Calls such as the one in this example need to be agreed on by the prosecutor and parent before they are made.)

The passage of time can work to the defense's advantage. Continuances are routinely requested. And the defense will usually waive the speedy trial requirement as well, slowing down the court process. The defense is hoping that your child's memories will become more distant and his presentation will be less emotional.

The defense attorney understands that postponing the trial can cause havoc with your emotions, especially if your family is geared up to appear in court. This roller-coaster experience can stack the cards in his or her direction because you can become exhausted. The Thompsons' trial date was changed three times! It was Phil's counseling that helped to make their situation more bearable.

BECOMING DETACHED

Although it can be a difficult pill to swallow, you must understand that you have very little control over what happens after you call the child abuse hot line. Your best bet is to funnel your energies in your family's direction, helping them as well as yourself cope during this stressful time. While it's easier said than done, try to let go of feeling personally responsible for punishing the alleged offender. Reconcile yourself to the fact that it is beyond your control.

Stress Busting

Discovering that your child has been molested can be one of your most unsettling and stressful experiences. Here are some suggestions to help change the direction of your thinking and calm your anxiety. They're intended to draw from your personal strengths and prepare you to become less affected by circumstances out of your control:

- Think about the fact that while there can be an overall improvement in your family's communication, things will not be exactly the same as before you learned of your child's abuse. With the right intervention, you and your child will grow from the experience. How you handle future stress as well as the importance you place on the small stuff may be different in the future.

- Examine your physical responses when you hear from one of your support team members or when you listen to your child expressing sadness. Does your body tense? Is your breathing affected? Make an effort to respond to your tension by drinking cold water, which can help you to relax. Then lace your fingers together, place them over your stomach, and take some deep breaths. Don't forget to exhale.

- Take advantage when you are alone to kick a taped box around your yard or work out with a punching bag.

- Establish "fun time" with your family, and go on a picnic or watch a movie. Be careful about what movie you choose, however. You don't want to trigger your child into feeling alarmed. Participate in recreational activities together, and keep things active by setting up a volley ball or basketball net in your yard.

- Drink warm milk and take a hot bath before bedtime. Stay in your favorite pajamas all day on Sunday. Eat your favorite comfort food, and make a meal out of desserts.

- Take yourself to a massage therapist.

- Sign up for an expressive art class such as pottery, painting, or dance.

- Keep a journal.

- Take walks, sign up for yoga classes, ski, run, bike, or swim. The late Fred Rogers, creator of *Mr. Rogers' Neighborhood,* said that he relaxed by taking a daily swim, which he viewed as essential to his sense of well-being.

- Examine your attitudes about your child's experience by answering the following questions:

What do I believe about my child's experience?

What do I tell myself about who I am because of my child's experience?

If I would like to tell myself something different, what would it be?

Write down your answers with your nondominant hand. You may be surprised, because using the nondominant hand sometimes accesses more authentic feelings.

Because they could see they were making progress through their counseling and stress relief practices, the Thompsons were able to tolerate their long wait. Scott was beginning to enjoy his outdoor activities again, and Janet and Bill were having less intense conversations. Try to let it be the same for you.

8

Understanding Grief Stages and Secondary Traumatic Stress

When parents learn about their child's abuse, they usually experience a grief reaction. Understandably, many caregivers grieve their children's lost innocence. Other parents grieve the violation itself. Still many grieve their loss of trust in others or "the system."

When you first hear that your child was molested, you can experience a range of emotion, such as numbing, rage, and shock. These emotions may cause you to feel as if you've taken a blow to the stomach. Their intensity can be overwhelming.

GRIEF STAGES

You and your family are working through a grief process that begins with numbing and denial and proceeds through anger, guilt and depression, bargaining, and acceptance. You'll come to recognize that these emotions don't always follow a uniform pattern.

Numbing and Denial

While they may appear to be okay on the outside, parents can feel numb, cold, and frozen on the inside after first hearing about their child's abuse. They may seem as if they're listening and can even ask questions. But their ability to understand all the information may be temporarily disrupted. They may misinterpret or remember only part of what has been said.

When Scott told his dad about the abuse, Bill calmly listened and under the circumstances responded very well. Yet he was thinking about the believability of Scott's disclosure because it was hard to wrap his mind around the truth. He was finding it difficult to visualize Mr. Webster as a sex offender. The older man seemed gentle and even meek. Bill's own camping experience as a boy had been positive, and he couldn't imagine that Scott's program wasn't perfect. It was also shocking for Bill to picture Mr. Webster molesting his son.

Other parents have shared their first reactions on learning of the abuse:

> "When I found out my father-in-law had molested my daughter, I was dumbstruck. I'd noticed he singled Jennifer out for some reason, but I had no idea it was for more than her kind personality."

> "Jimmy, our baby-sitter, was great with the kids. He was athletic, clean-cut, and seemed to be the 'All American' teenager. When my kids told us about Jimmy's sexually abusive behavior, I kept asking them if they'd confused him with someone else. I just couldn't believe it."

> "Thomas seemed like such a harmless man. He was everybody's good neighbor. We were all shocked when we discovered that his computer lessons were meant to lure kids into his house. You can't trust anyone nowadays."

> "*Numb* is the only way I can describe it. I just felt numb and a ringing in my ears. No one is prepared for this kind of information about your own child."

Shock and denial gets expressed in a number of ways. People can behave oddly and use poor judgment when trying to get at the truth behind their children's disclosures. The following reality check goes over some predictable but counterproductive reactions to avoid.

Reality Check 9: Behaviors to Avoid

✓ Grilling people, including your social worker, about the believability of your child's statements

✓ Guarding the disclosure information to the extent that it isn't helpful to your family or support team

✓ Arguing with the lawyers about the alleged offender statement

✓ Repeatedly questioning your child

✓ Ignoring the needs of your other children

✓ Physically moving away

✓ Minimizing the sexual abuse

✓ Refusing to talk about your child's abuse

✓ Refusing counseling

Anger

Bill and Janet were angry at different times after learning about Scott's abuse. Janet sobbed, and Bill hit golf balls. The couple felt betrayed and were badly shaken. Soon, rage replaced their milder anger, compelling Janet to cry uncontrollably and Bill to kick a chair. Other parents explain their feelings this way:

> "If my wife hadn't asked me for my gun, I'm afraid I would have shot the bastard. I wanted to kill him. He took everything from my family."

"I hoped that the person who molested Ann was experiencing hell in jail. Our own hell was back at home when we held her while she cried, comforted her after her nightmares, or found her huddled in the closet."

"I hated my husband after what he'd done to his stepdaughter, my only child. He hurt my baby, and I won't have anything to do with him or his worthless family."

"The Lord says you shouldn't hate nobody, but Lord how I hate that woman at my child's day care center. She pulled the wool right over my eyes, and now she'll pay."

Anger is a great motivator. It propels parents of molested children to report the abuse, remove their kids from dangerous situations, and provide comfort. However, anger can instigate impulsive and negative actions as well. The following reality check lists some of the less effective anger behaviors. Whatever you do, avoid them. Instead, count to ten, drink cold water, or take a walk.

Reality Check 10: Inappropriate Ways to Express Your Anger

✓ Calling the investigators names or giving them a hard time

✓ Fighting with family and friends

✓ Blaming everyone but the alleged perpetrator

✓ Expecting others to take action on your behalf when it's really your responsibility

✓ Becoming angry with your child when she doesn't "snap out of" her emotions

✓ Threatening to physically harm the alleged perpetrator or his family

✓ Excessively using drugs or alcohol

✓ Engaging in risky behaviors such as dangerous driving, playing with firearms, or gambling

✓ Excessively punishing your children

✓ Taking your anger out on your spouse or partner

✓ Writing angry letters to the editor of your local newspaper

✓ Stalking the alleged perpetrator

✓ Becoming angry with your therapist for not "fixing" the problem

Guilt and Depression

A well-known family therapist often remarked that feeling guilt seems to be a daily experience for parents. And by virtue of the fact they are parents, Bill and Janet's guilt soon escalated after their son's disclosure. Time and again, Janet asked Scott if he thought she was a good mom. Scott's mood sometimes dictated a positive or negative response. Bill kept his guilt to himself but demonstrated it through his generous gifts. Scott had a new fishing pole soon after his formal interview.

When their kids have been molested, parents should do their best to keep guilt at bay. Guilt stops people in their tracks and inhibits authentic behavior. Scott's folks could not have prevented the molestation. Most parents don't own crystal balls.

The sense that they had done something wrong didn't help Bill and Janet feel better. The sooner guilt is out of the picture, the sooner parents can resume their responsibilities and get on with parenting their kids. (Family guilt is further discussed in Chapter Eleven.)

Depression surfaces intermittently throughout the healing process, and some people are more susceptible to it than others. Most of the time, depression is a neural chemical-related condition, slowing down our minds and bodies. It's triggered by our genes, stress, and the feeling that we are powerless to control the bad stuff that happens. Often other disturbing memories surface and get thrown into the feeling pot, intensifying sadness, hopelessness, and guilt.

Bill and Janet experienced depression differently from each other: Bill spent longer hours in bed, and Janet cried more often, and she began to recycle a disturbing memory about a personal childhood incident.

Guilt and depression reactions are normal. Other parents share their comments:

> "I would cry after my daughter fell asleep at night. My anguish came out in wails and whimpers. I felt betrayed and helpless to make it better for her."

> "I felt so guilty about my son's abuse. I thought I should have interviewed his baby-sitter more thoroughly. Sometimes I just stared into space, absorbed in my self-loathing."

> "I kept everyone in the family busy. We went to the circus, out to dinner, to the movies—anything you can think of to keep my wife and me from thinking about our child's abuse. Slowing things down meant I'd feel bad."

> "I couldn't eat anything for days. My husband couldn't sleep. We were like two zombies in some kind of nightmare."

> "My husband began drinking again, and sometimes I didn't know where he was. He wouldn't talk about Shawn's abuse. I guess he was depressed."

> "I wanted to make it up to my daughter—the fact that my boyfriend tried something with her. I got her hair and nails done, and then we went out for dinner. She knew I felt guilty, but I couldn't bring myself to say anything."

The following reality check lists major symptoms of depression. As you review it, think about whether you've developed any of them. If three or more of these symptoms describe you, this is a signal of depression and needs attention.

Reality Check 11: Depression Symptoms

✓ Hopelessness

✓ Sadness

✓ Guilt

✓ Little or no appetite or eating excessive amounts of food

✓ Crying

✓ Mood swings

✓ Low self-esteem

✓ Irritability and impatience

✓ Physical aches and pains and recurring illnesses

✓ Disruption in sleep or sleeping too much

✓ Avoidance of normal activities

✓ Loss of enjoyment

✓ Absent-mindedness, distractedness, or preoccupation

✓ Anxiety

✓ Ongoing exhaustion

✓ Impulsiveness and explosiveness

✓ Compulsive worry and upset

✓ Excessive use of drugs or alcohol or prescription drugs

✓ Resumption of smoking

✓ Suicidal thoughts or plan

———————

Any thoughts of harming yourself need immediate attention!

Bargaining

Bargaining appears throughout the grief process. We bargain with God, our therapist, or our kids in order to try and control the situation. Sometimes we'll strike a bargain with ourselves to be better parents or spouses. "If I can just get through this, I promise to stop yelling, complaining, or badgering," we say.

Bargaining is one way to rationalize what has happened. It occupies us to the extent that we don't deal with the truth because the truth hurts. No amount of negotiating will make your child's experience go away. For example, shopping will not make her forget or get through her own grieving faster. Paying your therapy bill doesn't stop your therapist from asking you to work at your healing. And serving cake to the investigators will not control the outcome of the investigation.

When Janet and Bill were passing through their bargaining moments, they pressured themselves into unnecessary purchases and at times careless caregiving. The children stayed up later on school nights and weekends, ate junk food, and were granted permission more readily.

Parents will be preoccupied and distracted in the first weeks following their children's disclosure. Consequently, they bargain for personal time. Children are set before the television or play stations more often and sometimes left alone to make their own meals or complete adult chores.

Parents had this to say:

> "I tried to persuade our therapist that as long as Frank and I were at the sessions, my daughter didn't need to be in therapy. I wanted to protect Heather from any more disruptions in her life."

> "I didn't realize how neglected my other kids were while I was running Megan to all her meetings. They had to do too much and later rebelled."

> "I figured that if we moved away [from the community where we had been living], we'd forget about the whole miserable episode. It didn't work."

> "I tried to tell my husband that I didn't need an antidepressant. He didn't believe me, and after a while I didn't believe myself."

> "Sara still felt bad even after we painted her room and bought her new curtains. She wasn't going to get over her sexual abuse because we redecorated her room."

> "Refusing to discuss Andy's sexual abuse didn't make it go away. Finally, I was convinced that we would get through this if we all sat down and talked. But it wasn't easy."

> "I tried to tell the children that if we all put on smiles, we would feel a whole lot better. Over time, I could feel the stress of 'being cheerful' wearing on us."

> "I figured that her drug addiction had something to do with my daughter's earlier sexual abuse. But I didn't want to talk about that. I wanted her to fix her problem and forget about what happened."

Acceptance

Accepting the situation is one of the last stages in the grieving process. When family members have accepted the truth—that the sexual abuse happened and that it affected everyone—they have moved along in their healing. Getting to the stage of acceptance varies depending on each situation, as well as a person's willingness to work at feeling better. When you've reached the stage of acceptance, you have pretty much let go of any preconceived ideas about child sexual assault and have begun to learn from the experience. Throughout your family's recovery, you will begin to accept your child's abuse. For example, you may accept that she was molested but still need to accept that she was traumatized. Acceptance is continuous.

In accepting the fact that there are different stages of grief, Janet and Bill are working toward acceptance. Understanding these normal emotions can be reassuring and validating. What you're feeling now about your child's sexual assault is probably very normal. Under the circumstances, feeling abnormal is actually normal.

A sense of calm and well-being usually accompanies acceptance. As the Serenity Prayer reminds us, we try to accept the things we cannot change, demonstrate courage to change the things we can, and ask for wisdom to know the difference.

Parents discussed this stage when they shared their comments:

"I finally got to the point where I said, 'I'm giving this to God.' It helped."

"After feeling a whole bunch of intense emotions, I was too pooped to do anything but go with the flow."

"There came a time when I was less affected by what was happening in court. I had to rely on our system of government. Otherwise I would be a hypocrite."

"I guess seeing my daughter improve through therapy helped me change my mind and accept the fact that outside help does work."

"Sidney's abuser will get what's coming to him. What I now know is that I don't have to be responsible."

"Over time, I kind of grew into accepting that nothing could change the fact that my son was raped. No amount of drinking or fishing could stop the pain. It just had to work its way through me."

Chapter Sixteen goes into more detail on acceptance. For now, the following reality check lists a few acceptance behaviors and attitudes.

Reality Check 12: Acceptance Behaviors and Attitudes

✓ You don't hold your breath every time the attorney calls.

✓ You look forward to the next day.

✓ You've slowed down your reaction time by learning to breathe more deeply.

✓ You stop referring to your child as "the poor thing."

✓ You feel calmer.

✓ You realize you're not superhuman or immune to life's difficulties.

✓ You no longer fantasize about harming your child's molester.

✓ You stop writing angry letters in your head.

✓ You remember to smile.

✓ You remember to be grateful.

✓ You put your child back on a schedule.

✓ You don't feel guilty for saying no.

✓ You work well with your therapist.

✓ You have more patience.

✓ You eat and sleep better.

✓ Your concentration has returned.

✓ You exercise.

✓ You feel hopeful.

✓ You have a deeper understanding that you and your family will survive to flourish once again.

WORKING YOUR WAY THROUGH THE GRIEF STAGES

Grief doesn't follow a set protocol. Acceptance may happen after denial. You may never feel depressed. You could feel anger and never be numb. And the stages can be triggered all over again just when you think you're finished with them.

It's normal for the stages to creep in unexpectedly. Continue to see them as normal, without feeling as though there is one perfect way to get through your experience. If any of these stages threatens to get the best of you, seek help. Don't try to manage alone. And remember that when you work at it, the chances are slim you'll be experiencing your grief forever. *You will survive.*

In a strange way, working through grief can be a blessing. What you learn during the process can enrich your life and prompt you to appreciate what you already have. Take comfort in knowing there is help and that you will grow in wisdom.

UNDERSTANDING SECONDARY TRAUMATIC STRESS AND COMPASSION FATIGUE

It would be unusual if you aren't affected by your child's traumatic experience. In attempting to help, you vicariously experience the trauma second hand. Consequently, you can develop Secondary Traumatic Stress (STS), also called Compassion Fatigue.

While their conventional ideas about being "good parents" are challenged, caregivers are also thrown into intense and unfamiliar situations following their children's disclosures. The stresses brought about by these circumstances can be extreme and unrelenting. In a short while, parents can feel anxious and tense. Sleep and eating habits may be disrupted, and moods can become irregular.

STS symptoms often mirror acute stress, discussed in Chapter Four. (Another shared symptom is emotional exhaustion.) This condition emerges as a result of helping your child through this crisis. STS can surface suddenly, causing you to feel confused, helpless, and even isolated from other supporters such as your spouse.

Sometimes the symptoms are not related to real causes and can even breed irrational thinking, such as taking on excessive guilt about something you had no control over or feeling worthless and discouraged because something bad happened to your child.

STS can affect your work as well. If it is already stressful, this condition can add more pressure. One parent lost his job because his grief about his daughter's molestation spilled over to his work. And one mom reported that her ability to complete her work was deeply affected.

Researchers report that STS can affect people physically, emotionally, and behaviorally. Your personal relationships can be affected too. Watch for an increase in irritability, disinterest in normal activities, colds, high blood pressure, headaches, stomach problems, lost work, sleep disturbance, and loss of confidence. They are all signs reflecting an STS condition.

WORKING THROUGH SECONDARY TRAUMATIC STRESS

STS surfaces quickly and subsides more rapidly than other conditions such as posttraumatic stress. The key to working through your feelings is to understand that they're natural and will settle down when you pay them attention.

The more that Janet Thompson suppressed her anger toward Mr. Webster, the more she found herself dreaming about him at night. It had been grilled into her in her childhood that "nice" people don't express anger. Phil, her therapist, recommended that she write Mr. Webster a letter she wouldn't send, telling him exactly how she felt. When she read the letter aloud in a session with Bill, she was able to acknowledge her guilt and frustration. Afterward, she felt relief, and the nightmares diminished.

When you're especially sad or angry about your child's abuse, ask yourself, "How old do I feel right now?" By identifying an age, you may also be able to remember a personal traumatic experience that occurred at the age you've just identified. Write about the past experience or share it with your therapist, but try not to let it get blurred with your child's sexual assault. It's helpful to separate your child's past from your own in order to focus on getting through your child's experience.

Watch your diet, smoking, and beverage intake, including caffeine drinks and alcohol. Overindulgence in food and drugs can occur as a result of trying to numb distressing feelings and emotions, but they negatively affect your health.

Until you feel better, say no to any extra activities, and turn off your cell phone. Spend time with nature or get a massage. Talk to supportive friends, and go to bed earlier. Most important, keep your therapy appointments.

As you gradually control those controllable areas of your life, you will feel better. Remember that STS happens when people feel powerless to make things better for their kids. By virtue of the fact that you reported your child's abuse or otherwise supported her disclosure to someone else, you're empowering yourself to take control.

Over time, your STS symptoms will go away. Don't worry if on occasion they return, especially when you understand how quickly everyone can be triggered by association to their child's abuse. Unfortunately, life cannot be wrapped in a tidy package and pulled together with a bright bow.

THINGS GET BETTER

Don't be discouraged if you feel hopeless about your grief reactions or STS. Things get better! And your love and compassion for your child are reflected through these natural responses to her molestation.

Conversely, if you aren't moving through the grief stages and aren't suffering from compassion fatigue, don't pressure yourself to experience them. What matters most is how you support your child through her recovery. Chapter Nine will provide information to assist you in finding a therapist who can help you and your family move through this experience.

9

Working with a Counselor

Digesting your child's molestation is a tall order. Navigating through your emotions and getting perspective on the situation is challenging. Because sexual abuse is often traumatic for children and secondarily traumatic for their parents, it is important to get help as soon as possible. Studies have shown that people are most receptive to getting outside help when they are in crisis and children are best healed when there is immediate therapeutic intervention following their sexual assault.

During this crisis phase, your new therapist can offer insight into the investigation process and "reality check" your feelings. He or she can begin to forge a bond with your child and immediately offer helpful pieces of "homework" to do with your family between sessions. Therapy can also serve as a touchstone as you are guided to personal recognition and practice better family communication. And your therapist may prove to be your greatest advocate in court.

In some instances, particularly in cases of incest, families are court-ordered to enter and complete a specialized treatment program. These programs offer group as well as individual therapy. They're intended to monitor you and your family through reconciliation or permanent separation while teaching you better ways to build family communication and trust.

Whether or not you have been ordered to enter treatment, you and your family deserve to have your own coach as you try to reconcile something that doesn't make sense. It's practically impossible to get a grip on the situation if you don't have professional third-party input. Even therapists can't treat their own families. So don't feel insulted if your support team recommends you seek immediate help.

SELECTING A COUNSELOR

If you're fortunate, you will have some choice in choosing your therapist. The Thompsons were referred to Phil because he worked under contract with the Child Protection Team and was well trained in working with sexually abused children. Because of his affiliation with an agency, his fee was reduced. The situation worked well for everyone. But Bill and Janet weren't obligated to work with only Phil.

Some agencies are not able to provide treatment, but they will recommend psychotherapists. And there are different payment schedules for families. Don't choose a therapist based solely on fee. You can spend a good deal of wasted time with a less expensive person who doesn't have sufficient background in these matters. Experts have demonstrated by their postgraduate education and experience that they can put your family back on track.

Remember that a doctorate degree or medical license does not indicate someone is an expert in working with molested kids. Many people with a master's degree have more experience and training in this area. Training is key when identifying the right professional, and a large part of that training is geared to becoming skilled in treating trauma survivors:

- Licensed marriage and family therapists (LMFTs) have acquired specialized training in working with families. Many times they are qualified to address the sexual abuse issue as well.

- Licensed clinical social workers (LCSWs) may have been trained in working with sexually abused children and families.

- Licensed mental health counselors (LMHCs) have received more general counseling training but may have special postgraduate schooling too.

- Licensed psychologists (Ph.D.s or Psy.D.s) and psychiatrists (M.D.s) may or may not have received training in working with families as well as sexual abuse recovery.

Some families prefer to work with religious counselors. But unless they have received specialized training, they can be more effective as support persons who refer you to a specialist.

It's best to approach hiring a therapist from a consumer perspective. You are the customer and have a right to ask questions in order to determine a good match between you and your coach. In some communities, you may not have many choices, but the following reality check will help you ask the right questions.

Reality Check 13: Therapist Selection Questions

You may wish to ask the questions that follow over the telephone or in person. Most professionals will set up an initial consultation session that is intended to provide information and answer your questions. Because they want what's best for you and your child, they will determine their capability to work with you too.

The questions here will provide you with enough information to decide if you want to follow up with another appointment. Keep in mind that professionals should answer your questions without becoming defensive:

✓ How long have you been practicing?

Don't be put off by a young therapist with only a few years of experience. She may be better trained than an older, more experienced therapist who is unfamiliar with newer intervention techniques. Sometimes teenagers relate better to younger therapists as well.

✓ Could you please share your educational background?

Under ideal circumstances, the person working with your family should be a licensed mental health professional with postgraduate training in family therapy and trauma treatment.

✓ How long have you been working with children and families?

Be wary of therapists who haven't worked with children and families. In addition, you may relate better to therapists who are parents themselves.

✓ Where did you receive your sexual abuse treatment training?

At the postgraduate level, a therapist treating sexually molested children and their families should receive training at a family therapy institute plus course or seminar training with a recognized expert in the treatment of trauma. Course work includes identifying and treating trauma survivors, as well as understanding neural research. It is highly recommended that your therapist be certified in a neural biology technique that engages specific brain wave function, such as Eye Movement Desensitization Reprocessing (EMDR) or similar trauma intervention.

✓ How would you work with my child and our family?

Most therapists will want to spend time with you alone to obtain your child's physical and social history along with information on the sexual abuse allegation. You may have more than one session alone while she acquires this information. At that time, you will be asked to sign a release of information form so that she can speak to your support team as well.

Depending on your child's age and maturity, your therapist may take more time alone with you and your spouse than with your child. For example, you may spend more time if your child is very young because you will be receiving parenting techniques to try between sessions. Older children may use more alone time with the therapist, while your family will attend sessions once or twice a month. However it plays out, don't be surprised if you're asked to participate in specific communication or other relationship-building tasks during the week.

Your therapist may invite you to join a support group. Often, children benefit from group therapy as well.

In the beginning, your therapist may want to see you and your child often, perhaps twice a week. As time goes by, your meetings will be scheduled further apart.

Because treating trauma survivors entails reactivating portions of the brain, play therapy is often used in your young child's recovery. Play therapy can incorporate role play, working with sand or clay, painting or drawing, or even music and dance. Older kids respond well to role playing and expressive therapies as well.

During the course of treatment, the therapist may request to see family members individually, in selected pairings, or with extended family members. And don't be frustrated if you are asked to rephrase your comments and refrain from blaming people while you're in session.

Remember that therapy is not painless. There are very few people who enter into it without being in crisis.

Understand that surfacing past and current painful feelings is part of the process when it is used to prompt personal awareness and growth. Pleasant, superficial therapy is usually ineffective.

Therapists approach their work in different ways. And most of the time, the approach suits their personality. Soft-spoken therapists can be extremely helpful, as can bolder, more provocative ones. There is no one right way. Their work is to elicit honest feelings, while making you aware of your anxiety, strengths, and effective ways to make family connections, as well as support your child through his recovery.

✓ What about my child's confidentiality?

By law, licensed mental health professionals are required to keep your child's treatment confidential unless you have signed release of information forms. Under certain circumstances, your therapist may be ordered to divulge her session notes with the alleged perpetrator's attorney and the judge.

Remember that it's important for your therapist to be included as one of the support team members. Discretion is used in divulging frivolous material such as rumored information, but it's important to share relevant information, especially during the investigation and prosecution stages.

Your case coordinator will explain and have you sign any needed consent forms at your first meeting.

✓ Are you comfortable with or experienced in reviewing videotape disclosures and videotaping therapy sessions?

Any therapist who works with sexually abused children should be familiar with videotaping protocol and understand the most effective methods for the use of videotaping in the context of a therapeutic session. If you interview a professional who is unfamiliar with videotaping, simply tuck the information away as you continue to assess your compatibility.

✓ Are you familiar with preferential as opposed to situational sex offenders?

This question draws out therapists' knowledge about sex offenders and enlightens you about their competence to work with your family (see Chapter One).

✓ Do you recommend medication intervention for traumatized children?

In the past, very little attention was paid to medication when therapists were treating sexually abused children. More recently, medication therapy has become a consideration when therapists are doing their assessments. Most of the time, children do not need medication, but an experienced and knowledgeable therapist never rules out medication intervention without first assessing a number of factors. A therapist who immediately refers you or your child for medication evaluation before thoroughly obtaining a social or physical history is assuming too much too soon. Remember that medication intervention should never be the sole form of treatment. Studies show that psychotherapy needs to accompany medication intervention. In addition, children on medication must be reviewed and/or reevaluated regularly by a qualified child and adolescent psychiatrist (who is a medical doctor), not a family practitioner (who is also a medical doctor).

✓ Do you recommend any reading materials that can help us get through this situation?

Your therapist should be able to recommend some helpful books or may even have a lending library in her office.

✓ Is my child going to be psychologically tested?

Chances are that your child will be given a simple trauma response scale by her therapist that registers how she's been affected. In some cases, your therapist may refer your child for more in-depth testing with a licensed psychologist if there are extenuating circumstances (for example, if she suspects your child has a learning problem). Psychological testing by a licensed psychologist can validate what your therapist suspects are the emotional effects of your child's abuse too.

If you are involved in a lawsuit with the perpetrator or are going through a custody battle and your child has made a disclosure about your former spouse, you may be required to complete psychological tests as well.

Further Considerations

If you sense that the therapist isn't comfortable or forthcoming with information, contact someone else. Defensiveness about answering your questions also indicates an inability or unwillingness to admit mistakes or deal with your emotions.

Your therapist's reputation is important too. If other support team members think she can do a good job, she most likely can. Sometimes support teams haven't had the opportunity to meet other specialists. Go with your instincts if they do not know the therapist you have contacted.

Keep in mind that some children relate better to males or females. Ask your child whom he would prefer to see. And think about your preference as well.

> ## Understanding Eye Movement Desensitization Reprocessing: One Neural Biology Technique
>
> Eye Movement Desensitization Reprocessing (EMDR) was developed in the latter part of the last century to help alleviate distress associated with traumatic memories. Traumatic memories are accessed within the trauma survivor by stimulating the brain through lateral eye movements, tapping, or audio stimulation. When these memories are surfaced, more positive associations and beliefs about traumatic experiences can be substituted.
>
> Research has demonstrated EMDR's effectiveness in reducing or eliminating problems that originate after a distressing experience. (It does not alleviate symptoms arising in physiological disorders such as schizophrenia or bipolar disorder.) EMDR has been helpful in reducing the level of distress in traumatized children. As with all other therapeutic interventions, the technique must be administered by a licensed mental health professional who is certified in EMDR.

WORKING EFFECTIVELY WITH YOUR THERAPIST

Work with a therapist who puts your child's welfare first but has the ability to use discretion when it comes to establishing professional boundaries. In other words, your therapist will have the capacity to make and keep appointments, she won't get overwhelmed by your emotions or caught up in your problem, and she won't share her own troubles with you. (However, she may use a brief anecdotal story to get a point across.) Your therapist will also draw the line when it comes to being accessible. She will have an emergency contact number, but she won't give you her home phone.

The following reality check shares some helpful pointers in making the most of your therapy experience.

Reality Check 14: Realistic Expectations About Counseling

✓ You will need to be honest with your therapist. Share all your family history and sexual abuse facts. Be open about your feelings. And keep in mind that your therapist is not there to judge.

✓ Understand that a therapist won't be placing labels on you or your child, except to give your or his condition a diagnosis if one is needed. You won't be called "crazy," and by law information must be confidential. Your therapist won't be sharing your case at the dinner table.

✓ Be aware that there is no optimal number of sessions. You could meet 3 or 103 times. And there is no magical formula when it comes to an end. You may opt to renew your sessions again when your child passes through another developmental stage or if you get stuck recycling poor communication habits.

✓ When you sign a release form, make sure it identifies to whom the information is being released.

✓ Your therapist cannot make your decisions for you.

✓ Don't expect your therapist to put up with foul language or threats. Her office and profession must be respected.

✓ You may have to pay out-of-pocket expenses for therapy, and the fees vary. In working out a payment arrangement, try to remember that if she's in private practice, a therapist must pay all her expenses. In addition, she worked long and hard to earn her credentials.

✓ Having a therapist doesn't give you permission to "let it all hang out." In other words, control demonstrations of affection and other behaviors with your family when you are in session.

✓ You may feel exceedingly vulnerable and embarrassed after an especially revealing session. This is normal. Resist the temptation to cancel your next therapy appointment.

✓ Because your therapist is human, she will make at least one mistake. She may forget your husband's name or say something dumb, for example. If she apologizes, let it go. And try not to react too strongly to your disappointment. By her role, she can seem like an authority figure. So while you may have the urge, don't rebel.

✓ Let your therapist know when you're disappointed or angry. These moments are opportunities to learn effective ways to deal with your feelings.

✓ Your family may experience another crisis during your treatment. Allow your therapist to help you work through it in a positive way.

✓ Do your homework assignments. Many families express disappointment in their therapy, but ignore the fact that they didn't follow through on any of their therapist's suggestions.

✓ Go to therapy even when you think there's nothing to say. There is *always* something to say.

✓ Remember that your therapist will probably not
become a family friend in the sense of sharing dinner or
a Sunday barbecue. Your therapist must maintain a professional distance so that she can do her best work.

THERAPY CAN MAKE A BIG DIFFERENCE

Therapy can make a difference in your child's life, and it can support you on the way to healthier family communication. For Janet
and Bill, it made a big impact because they were guided by a skilled
professional who led them through their family's recovery.

Your therapist can provide practical information as well as be a
pivotal force in your family's healing. Chapter Ten focuses on what
you can do to promote your child's recovery as well.

10

Helping Your Child Recover

Helping your child recover from her sexual molestation is one of your most important tasks. Seeing her therapist is helpful, but structured therapy provides only a portion of what she needs in order to heal. Because your child spends so much more time with you, numerous opportunities abound when you can support her recovery.

Earlier traumatic experiences and therapeutic intervention have a lot to do with how children are affected by their sexual abuse. Had Scott Thompson experienced previous trauma such as a serious car accident or family divorce, his trauma symptoms might have been more acute, especially if he had received no help. In addition, had his parents not responded immediately to his need, he could potentially develop more serious problems later.

Children pass through confusion, reorientation, and integration phases as they grieve their abuse. For example, confusion accompanies the numbing and denial grief stage.

During this first phase, their overwhelming feelings are anxiety and fear, especially for their personal safety. They may be hypersensitive to sudden noises or abrupt routine changes. Excessive worry about punishment from the alleged perpetrator, family, or friends is common. Children may be excessively clingy, distracted, or irritable, and they often feel guilty or like damaged goods.

Children can be confused and disoriented in the initial phase. They need to be reoriented so that they can understand they're okay, not responsible, and certainly not damaged.

During their second, or reorientation, phase, kids may feel depression, sadness, and anger. They will work at striking bargains with pivotal people, such as their parents. For instance, they won't discuss their feelings in order to avoid upsetting their mom or dad, or they'll pretend nothing happened when they see their date rapist at a school function.

In the reorientation phase, children have opportunities to learn new skills about coping as well as rebuild self-esteem. During this time, they can be shown positive ways to express themselves and be reassured that expressing emotion is a normal human experience. How you handle yourself as a parent is very important because your child will often mimic your coping attitudes and behaviors. Try to be open to learning new stress-management techniques while encouraging your child to do the same.

When they've entered into the final, or integration, phase following their sexual assault, kids generally think of it as a sad event that is part of their personal history. If parents and other helpers have done their work, children will feel more empowered, understand they weren't responsible, and view the experience as a springboard for giving their personal suffering meaning.

As your child's most powerful helper, remember that feeling safe is the largest issue for your child after her abuse. Remember too that you have a responsibility to facilitate her healthy growth and renewed confidence. The following reality check provides suggestions to assist you in helping her feel safe and supporting her toward positive self-perception.

Reality Check 15: Helping Your Child Feel Safe and Supporting Her Toward Positive Self-Perception

✓ Resume your child's normal routine as soon as possible. Mandated appointments and the extra activity prompted by her disclosure are disruptive, so try to put your child back on her usual schedule.

✓ Be careful how you enter her room, give direction, and speak. Loud, sudden voices may be startling and scary to her. And when she is contemplating trying anything new, explain it thoroughly.

✓ Ask your child to tell you when she's feeling nervous in her body. Then you and she can come up with a plan to help her feel less jumpy. Don't forget to have her drink cold water.

✓ Ask your child if there is anything worrying her. You can ask, "Do you feel safe right now?" Do everything in your power to address her concerns.

✓ Ask your child if there is anything in her possession that helps her feel safe, such as a necklace, lucky penny, or favorite picture. Encourage her to keep it close at hand. Or you can get her a "lucky" stone or feather, and tell her to keep it with her when she feels nervous or scared.

✓ Change the locks in your house, and put a night light in her room if it helps your child feel more secure. Let her help you do this work.

✓ Ask your child if there are any windows in her bedroom that appear scary at night. Come up with an idea together about how you can cover the window or move her furniture. (One young sexual abuse survivor was terrified at night because the large tree limbs near her second-story window scraped against the pane. She was frightened that the alleged perpetrator, who had yet to be arrested, was going to enter her room through the window.)

✓ Give your child a beeper to carry, make sure she has your cell phone number, and ask your teenager to always carry enough money to make a phone call or take a cab or bus home.

✓ Ask your child if she is having bad dreams. Follow up by asking her to discuss or draw them for you.

✓ Pay attention to your child's television and computer game viewing. Triggers or mental associations to the abuse abound, so curbing scary or dramatic material may be best for the time being.

✓ Help your child feel comfortable by accompanying her on her first outings after the abuse. For example, Bill Thompson went camping with Scott to help reorient him to outdoor life. Some parents walk their kids into the school building or stay to the end of athletic practice.

✓ Help your child take risks by signing up for a new class or exploring nature together.

✓ Spend some time together finger painting, coloring, or tossing around clay.

If your child draws anything particularly worrisome, show it to her therapist.

✓ Engage your family in board games, and try to make it part of family night. This is a wonderful way for your child to feel surrounded by people she loves.

✓ Engage in some form of exercise together. Walking, dancing, riding bikes, and swimming are powerful depression fighters.

✓ Praise your child for her courage.

✓ Be careful not to overreact if your child resists your "safety" suggestions or discloses other upsetting information. For example, be patient if she has trouble being alone, and don't let her see you cry if she tells you she feels as if she did something wrong.

✓ Use humor to accentuate the positive, and remember that children are resilient.

MANAGING YOUR CHILD'S ANGER

Anger is an important emotion that needs to be addressed during your child's recovery. Here are some examples.

When Your Child Thinks You Could Have Prevented Her Abuse

At some point, the issue of your being unavailable during your child's molestation may surface. Unless you address it directly, your child may act out her anger in a number of self-harming ways. Use your therapy session for this discussion, or choose a time to bring up the topic when you're alone together and not pressured by other responsibilities.

Don't be afraid to ask your child if she thinks you could have stopped the abuse from occurring. More than likely, she'll say no, because she doesn't want to hurt your feelings, but she will feel relieved that you asked. Continue by saying that almost all kids think their parents should have been there to stop it, even if it was impossible. Tell her that you're very sorry you weren't there, and if she's mad, you understand. Then ask how you can help her now.

When Your Child Is Just Plain Angry

It's pretty normal for your child to be angry following her molestation. Talk about it with her, but be careful that you don't indulge irrational beliefs or behaviors. Instead, try these suggestions:

• Remind your child that her body will feel hot and tense before she explodes, so teach her about being aware of her tension so that she doesn't have to wear herself out by exploding. Let her know that she can take some deep breaths and focus on directing them to her tension spots. She can also imagine drawing in a favorite color as she inhales and further imagining the color spreading throughout her body as she exhales. Also ask her to tell you or her teacher when she feels her body getting tense.

• Teach your child words to express how she feels.

• Teach your child to understand that some things that happened in the past can affect how we behave now. For instance, if she was bumped in the hallway before school, she could feel jumpy or edgy when the teacher asks her a question later. You can use this example to discuss the fact that being molested can affect how we feel later as well.

• Teach your child to understand that her behavior can create positive or negative consequences. She can still be angry about what happened, but she needs to let you know in order for you to help her express her anger in ways that do not get her in trouble.

• Refrain from making negative comments when your child shows her temper.

• When your child is upset, ask her to tell you why. Then repeat back exactly what she said. Don't interpret; just repeat. Follow up by asking what she thinks should happen next. This exercise works toward diffusing her anger.

• Don't allow the anger to go unnoticed. Disrupt it as soon as possible, and retrain her about healthy anger expression. Kicking a taped box is great. So is going to a batting cage or beating a drum. Don't let your teenager drive when she's upset, and give her time alone to cool down.

• If your child is small and acting up, place her on a couch or chair for a five-minute time-out. Don't put her somewhere else like a bedroom. Keep her in sight so that she doesn't feel abandoned.

- Remember to reward positive behavior. Notice and comment on it.
- Notice how you express your own anger. Role modeling is a powerful influence.

HELPING YOUR CHILD THROUGH STORYTELLING

As you continue to support your child through her healing, you can use storytelling to get across powerful messages that address her problem, help her problem-solve, and view herself in a positive light.

Metaphorical or symbolic stories are extremely helpful when kids aren't ready to discuss their abuse or when they become overly anxious as the subject comes up. Storytelling speaks to children's unconscious, emphasizing their strengths while bypassing their conscious resistance. Stories are also very calming.

Human beings are affected by stories. The story of the Little Engine That Could resonates with almost everyone because it describes how working to the best of one's ability can bring about positive outcomes. Our ancestors knew the power of the spoken word as they passed down creation stories and heroic tales.

After Bill Thompson learned about Scott's abuse, he made an effort to share family stories about members who overcame their problems. Because Scott's grandfather had been an immigrant, Bill talked about Grampa's challenges as he journeyed to America. Bill was careful to include problem-solving solutions in his yarns and mindful about telling them while he and Scott were going about their usual routines such as driving or clearing the dishes. The stories had a powerful effect on his son, and soon Scott was overheard passing them along to his younger sister, Beth. Following is one of the stories that Bill told.

Grampa Thompson's Scary Journey

Once upon a time, Grampa Thompson, or Scotty, as everyone called him, decided to take a big ship across the ocean. Grampa Thompson was a boy back then and had never been near the water before, let alone on a big boat. He was very nervous, but of course didn't want anyone else to know.

The day he started on his journey, his mother and father walked him down to the pier and gave him four gold coins. "These coins will get you on your way son," they said. "Remember to keep them safe."

As he waved goodbye to his parents, Scotty noticed that as the ship went farther out to sea, it began to rock back and forth. All the rolling made him a little nervous and a lot sick. He thought that if he went to his cabin, he would feel better. But his cabin was at the bottom of the boat, and as he went deeper and deeper down, it became darker and darker. By this time, Grampa Scotty was feeling very ill.

When he opened his cabin door, he saw that his cabin mates were three other men. Two looked to be his age, and another seemed much older. The two younger ones introduced themselves, and soon Scotty was telling them about his journey and the four gold coins in his pocket. The ship continued to toss and turn as they talked. All three of the young men were feeling very, very seasick.

The older man, named Hawthorne, had been silent for a long time, but he began to speak. "I know how to make you all feel better," he said, "but I need four gold coins so that I get all the proper ingredients for my special medicine."

None of the young men knew that seasickness goes away in time; they thought they would be sick forever. They were that sick! Scotty was the only one traveling with money, so he very sadly offered his gold coins to the older man. When Hawthorne left with the gold coins, his new friends thanked Scotty for his kindness. They were hoping that Hawthorne would soon return with the medicine to make them feel better.

As night fell, the man didn't return, so the three young men decided to find him. When they went up to the deck, they discovered Hawthorne playing cards and betting Scotty's money! Hawthorne had lied. There was no medicine in sight! Now Scotty felt even worse. He blamed himself for losing his parents' gift, and he felt depressed and betrayed. His friends silently filed downstairs to the cabin.

Yet Scotty was smart and clever. Long ago, he had learned the same card game Hawthorne was playing now. He had been taught by the card-playing expert in his village. The expert had given him good advice and told Scotty that playing cards took luck but mostly skill. And although Scotty felt terrible, he knew he could beat Hawthorne at his own game.

Meekly, Scotty asked the older man if he could play cards. All the men laughed at the bold young man. But Hawthorne, thinking that there was more money in Scotty's pockets, agreed.

Scotty took his lucky medal from around his neck and placed it on the table. He told Hawthorne that since he had no more money, his silver medal was all he could wager. Eyeing the beautiful chain, Hawthorne nodded.

Scotty played his cards just right, and soon he won all his money back. Hawthorne was angry because he was outsmarted by a boy. But the other passengers on the ship were impressed by Scotty's courage and knowledge. Word spread about his victory over the tricky older man.

Soon the seas calmed, and the ship once again sailed along smoothly. As the days passed, Scotty made friends with many more people, who asked him to teach them how to play the card game. The young man knew that when he reached his new country, he would be honest and courageous but careful too. And sure enough, that's just how things happened.

Bill thought that sharing a story about outsmarting a tricky person was a good message to send his son. In Scott's case, a scheming person had tried to use him as well. And in the end, Grampa Scotty outsmarted his thief and came out on top. Without directly discussing Scott's molestation, Bill sent a strong signal that his son could get through his ordeal with flying colors.

Pulling Together a Story

Sharing a story with your own child isn't hard because you can draw from stories already familiar to her. Simply insert one of your child's favorite TV or movie characters as the main character, and you're off and running. If you'd rather make up a special healing story for your child, keep these simple steps in mind:

- Make the story similar to your child's experience, but don't use the same names or directly address the molestation. Remember that your child will know exactly what you're doing without your being specific.

- The main character symbolically represents your child and should be a lovable character. Depending on what current popular character is special to your child, use it. And make its gender the same as hers.

- Use a symbol to represent the problem, whether it's a person, natural catastrophe, or a terrible accident. For example, you could say a terrible storm created an awful unstoppable tornado inside the main character.

- Highlight the problems that occurred because of the situation. In Scotty's story, he was sad, sick, and felt betrayed.

- Emphasize the main character's strengths. For instance, Scotty was smart and clever.

- Describe how the main character overcomes the problem. It doesn't have to be detailed. You can simply say something like, "When the princess fell asleep, she dreamed that a wizard whispered a special formula in her ear. When she awakened, she remembered the formula and knew just what to do. Soon her life turned around, and the sun began to shine again on her beautiful kingdom."

- If you use a helper messenger such as the wizard in the previous point, it should be someone or something your child likes.

- Emphasize your child's mastery of the problem by saying something like, "Before too long, things were back to normal in Wonder Woman's world. And Wonder Woman knew that her strength and skill had a lot to do with making it all happen."

- You will intuitively know how to make the story fit with your culture and your child's upbringing,

especially when you use a familiar story setting. She
will also resonate with your phrases and language.

Sharing the Story

There are different ways to share your healing message. One way is
to record it on an audiotape so your child can listen to it before bedtime. Sharing it in person is always a great way to connect with your
child as well. And telling the story when your family is all together
doesn't single your child out as different.

If your child is not feeling safe, she won't be able to hear the
story. Driving in your car or sitting comfortably on your couch are
settings that provide golden opportunities. Settling in a safe place
prepares your child at the unconscious level to take in the message.

Here are some suggestions for when you record your story:

- Tell your child she is not being hypnotized.

- Tell her that she can turn the tape off at any time, and
  it's not important if she pays strict attention.

- Invite her to let you know if the story was fun to
  listen to.

- Ease your child into the story. Begin by asking her to
  take a deep breath and exhale slowly.

- Convey the message that you were more than happy to
  make a story tape and that you are very proud of her.

- Begin your story with the phrase, "Once upon a
  time . . ."

- Keep the stories on the tape short if your child is
  young. But be sure to put more than one story on
  the tape.

- If your tape is for an adolescent, strongly caution her
  not to drive or operate any machinery while listening.

- Let her know she can share the tape with anyone.

- Remember to sound as though you're enjoying telling the story. Work at not sounding forced or stressed. Children of all ages like to hear the words *good*, *great*, *awesome* or *"you're on your way!"* on the tape. Keep it upbeat.

The Power of Stories

Alhough Janet Thompson's stories weren't as creative as her spouse's, she taped several heroic tales for Scott so that he could play them when he was agitated or preparing for a challenge, such as appearing in court. The story of Hercules was a favorite. Although Scott wasn't one to let his parents know everything, he did tell them that he played the tape before he fell asleep. Even Brad, Scott's older brother and roommate, remarked they "weren't so bad."

Symbolic healing stories can boost your child's confidence and get her moving forward. They're subtle and nonintrusive. After all, using a key is much more effective when opening doors.

Chapter Eleven explores the issue of family guilt following your child's sexual abuse.

11

The Impact on Family Members

Your child's sexual assault has an impact on the entire family. In the case of the Thompsons, all five family members were confronted with an "elephant in their living room." The circumstances created a disruption in their daily lives, and the topic was awkward for them to discuss.

Guilt continues to play a role in how family members behave with one another. Bill and Janet were unknowingly demonstrating their guilt when they consistently gave Scott the benefit of the doubt and indulged his moods.

Their behavior did not go unnoticed by the other children, who were very aware that Scott was given special treatment. At age seven, Beth was not accustomed to Scott's getting so much attention, and seventeen-year-old Brad wondered what the fuss was about.

Because their folks explained the abuse situation in the first family therapy session, they tried to understand. But for different reasons, both Beth and Brad felt resentment and guilt. Brad felt guilty about having had a great camping experience and wondered why Scott had been targeted for abuse. Beth felt guilty because she had been taught by her Sunday school teacher that when bad things happen to other people, she needed to feel bad for them too.

As weeks went by, Beth and Brad found themselves giving in to all the special demands pertaining to Scott's experience. Some of them included going to therapy and putting up with Scott's temper.

They resented the fact that it was interfering with their lives yet felt guilty for feeling resentful.

In spite of their best intentions, the children acted on their feelings. Beth began whining and complaining. She clung to her mother and reported feeling sick so that she could stay home and spend more time with her mom. Her strategy worked to some extent because it did buy her more time at home. Unfortunately, Janet wasn't as patient or fun to be around because she was distracted. Beth's behavior also annoyed her parents. It didn't occur to them until they began therapy to ask their daughter what she was feeling and how the "elephant" affected her as well.

Brad, never open about his feelings, withdrew from the family even more. He spent extra time with his friends, broke curfew, and let his grades slip. His parents seemed unavailable for the moment, and like any other normal teenager, Brad took the opportunity to spread his wings. Any resentment he felt toward Scott was put aside while he spent more time in clubs and at friends' houses.

His anger surfaced when Janet and Bill were too preoccupied to fill out some of his college application forms. Other college discussions were put on hold until Scott's investigation was settled. Brad was eagerly anticipating going away to school, and his brother's incident put a damper on his ability to get the ball rolling.

Scott, the middle child, was not happy about being molested. Strangely, he was not sad to get some focused attention either. It was a mixed bag: he felt bad about his abuse and guilty that he felt good about getting attention. It was a relief to hear Phil discuss this topic in therapy.

Janet and Bill felt pulled in all directions. In spite of Scott's circumstance, they still had to get Beth to soccer practice and Brad's curfew problem under control. To add to their problems, Bill's mother was in the process of moving to assisted living, and Janet's sister was going through a divorce. As a couple, they wondered when they would ever have alone time again. Yet even when there was a little breathing space, they both discussed Scott's case rather than other topics. And going out for a quiet dinner alone seemed to provoke too much guilt.

DEALING WITH YOUR FEELINGS

The reactions of the Thompson family were normal. Talking about their feelings in their counseling sessions with Phil provided a safe forum for discussion along with a lot of relief. As Phil stated, "Monsters don't live in the light!"

If you let your feelings, especially guilt, progress to the point where you become overwhelmed, you will get burned out and be ineffective as a parent. Continuing to feel guilty also stops your recovery progress and can add to your child's perception of being damaged goods.

Parents here share how their child's abuse affected their families:

"After the abuse, my whole family kind of fell apart. I didn't realize that I had always been the force holding it together. When all of my energies went to helping my child, the family couldn't keep going without my leadership. My daily routine changed to focus on Steve and his needs. That disrupted the routine of the whole family. I felt guilty about neglecting my other children, yet at the same time I felt helpless to manage my life in a way that included them all."

"Because I was a single parent, I felt I was spread painfully thin during this crisis. My attentions were focused on helping the legal system punish my daughter's abuser. I felt guilty that I hadn't protected her from this man and wanted to make up for what I felt I had neglected to do. In the process, I was trying to work and supervise my other child, who had been diagnosed as hyperactive. I knew he was not getting the attention and help he needed. It was a pretty rough time."

"My husband molested our daughter, and the authorities told me that he must get out of our home or I couldn't keep custody.

My husband and I had been married for eighteen years, and I was still in love with him. I wanted to believe he was telling the truth when he claimed he had never touched Jill. But what Jill said seemed to be true. At first, I resented her for disclosing. Then I felt guilty for being resentful because I knew I had to protect her. I felt very torn between my loyalties to each of them. It was the worst time of my life."

"When our only child was molested, I felt that I should have protected him more. To cover my guilt, I began spending all my free time with him, to the point of neglecting my wife, who was having real problems over what happened as well. It nearly destroyed our marriage. When we needed each other the most, I withdrew from her. I'm lucky that we had a good counselor who helped me put things into perspective."

"When my daughter reported the football player who attacked her after school, her younger brother was beaten up by some of his friends and warned to have her drop the case. They said that none of us would be safe anymore. It was a terrible time, and my kids ended up going to another high school. My daughter felt guilty for her brother's assault, and I felt guilty that I couldn't protect either one of them."

ANOTHER COUNSELING BENEFIT

Phil, the Thompsons' family therapist, recognized their feelings of guilt and resentment. Through his training and experience, he was able to assist them in expressing themselves while normalizing their feelings. After his first meeting with Janet and Bill, he had an idea about how to go about addressing these issues.

When Phil spoke with Janet, he could see she was examining her own ideas about what she expected of herself as a mom. He made a mental note to question her further and was mindful to comment on her strengths.

Bill's guilt was largely the result of thinking that he let Scott down because he was unable to be protective. He also felt guilt for wanting to physically harm Mr. Webster. As a strict practitioner of his faith, Bill felt guilty that he couldn't "turn the other cheek."

When Phil spoke with Scott alone, he was pleased to see that in spite of his experience, Scott behaved like a normal nine year old. But he noted that Scott's guilt was attached to shame; he felt that he had prompted Mr. Webster's behavior.

It became clear to Phil in the family session that Brad and Beth held resentments toward their brother and at the same time were feeling guilty. He observed Beth's clinging behavior and Brad's aloofness.

Understandably, the family, while generally comfortable with each other, was awkward around the issue of Scott's abuse. They didn't have the words to describe their feelings and didn't know how they were supposed to behave. There was considerable tension during the early family sessions.

Phil explained that guilt and resentment were normal under the circumstances. In fact, he mentioned that guilt is a positive feeling: it relates to having a conscience and understanding right from wrong. In the case of Mr. Webster, he *should* feel guilt. Yet, he continued, guilt as it relates to the Thompsons' experience stops them from being spontaneous and open with each other. Guilt and resentment drag people down and inhibit their ability to be natural. It doesn't accomplish anything.

Phil went on to say that getting stuck with guilty feelings prevents people from taking responsibility for making things different. He pointed out to Janet and Bill that indulging Scott was an attempt to erase their own guilt. Nevertheless, it would continue to surface. Openly discussing their feelings in the appropriate settings would lessen their anxiety and move them forward. For example, they could tell Scott that they were sad and angry about the sexual assault and ask what they could do to help him feel better, thus taking action and demonstrating their concern. Finally, Phil pointed out that attending their counseling sessions was another responsible behavior.

Phil reassured Scott that Mr. Webster was at fault and drove home the message using a symbolic healing story. Certified in Eye Movement Desensitization Reprocessing, he effectively used the technique with his young client. Scott was reporting that he didn't feel so responsible.

In family sessions, Beth's fears about also being harmed were calmed, and Brad was able to admit he felt guilty for not being victimized. Phil then drew out their sadness about their brother's experience. Both had an opportunity to grieve as well as share their opinions.

Alone again with Janet and Bill, Phil recommended reading material that addressed Bill's religious dilemma and outlined realistic parenting expectations as well as suggesting date nights for the couple.

DEALING WITH THE ELEPHANT IN YOUR LIVING ROOM

Unless your family lives apart, you will all be affected by your child's molestation. And while it's one more thing to deal with, continue to check in with family members to see how each one is coping. Remember that eventually life does return to normal, and routines are resumed.

Chapter Twelve looks at healing your family through strengthening communication.

Strengthening Family Communication

The stress caused by your child's molestation can affect how family members express their feelings and communicate their needs. If you've been pretty good at getting your messages across in the past, you may be unsettled by the awkwardness you feel now. If your family communication is already fragile, the extra pressure caused by the abuse can accentuate the existing problem.

Crisis brings opportunities for personal growth, and if you're willing to work at it, family communication can be enhanced through counseling. Sometimes, however, there are situations where people have been under stress for so long that they aren't aware communication has broken down. The following reality check shares common signs.

Reality Check 16: Family Communication Breakdown Signs

✓ Individual and family problems are not discussed or resolved.

✓ If problems are discussed, they are prompted by anger and expressed in angry ways.

✓ Parents or caregivers spend more time away from each other than they did in the past.

✓ Children become secretive.

✓ Families participate in distracting activities such as watching television or playing video games.

✓ One or both parents work to excess.

✓ Children and youth use force to express their anger.

✓ Parents don't take time to discuss feelings or resolve issues with each other.

✓ One or more family members indulges in binge eating.

✓ The parents' sexual patterns are disrupted.

✓ Overt avoidance occurs when sensitive topics are introduced.

✓ One or more family members uses drugs or alcohol to excess.

✓ Children and youth are not appropriately disciplined.

✓ A family member threatens suicide.

✓ School grades dip.

CHALLENGING OLD COMMUNICATION HABITS

Every family argues. Working toward the resolution of problems is challenging as well as a normal part of family living. The way in which arguments are resolved is a determining factor in identifying a healthy family.

Many adults did not learn coping skills and healthy communication in childhood. Perhaps the freedom to express oneself was not an option. In some families, it can be viewed as weakness. Consequently, guessing substitutes for authentic disclosure. It's not healthy. Believing someone should know what we feel is magical thinking. Not even our closest loved ones magically know what we need. Breaking through these belief barriers is critical in creating human connections.

The classic example of strong, silent men, characterized by actors such as Arnold Schwarzenegger and Clint Eastwood, has led people to adopt some pretty self-destructive beliefs and behaviors. The idea that individuals don't need other people is absurd, especially if they're in relationships. It may look convincing in movies, but it's unrealistic in the real world.

Women too have had some unrealistic role models. In the past, there were portrayals of women who gracefully cared for their homes and families without making demands on anyone. These updated heroines now manage full-time demanding careers and busy families. But for many women, the ability to express their personal needs is still a challenge.

THE THOMPSONS' EXPERIENCE

Bill and Janet Thompson considered themselves to be fairly open with one another. Prior to Scott's disclosure, they had mostly minor communication problems, and they worked at relating with one another: Janet frequently read self-help books, and Bill participated in a men's group at church.

Following Scott's disclosure, their communication took a downturn. When Bill began to brood alone in his workroom, Janet hoped he would snap out of his mood. She began to feel frustrated because her efforts to draw him out weren't working.

Although Bill expressed anger and rage a few times after learning about Scott's abuse, he immediately regained his composure and silence. Janet cried daily. She was more than eager to discuss her feelings and consequently took the lead when it came to speaking with authorities as well as to Brad and Beth. When she asked Bill how he felt about Webster's molesting his son, Bill blew up. "How do you *think* I feel!" he shouted, and stomped out of the room.

Janet and Bill felt differently about other issues as well. While Janet wanted to begin counseling as soon as possible, Bill was resistant. He was basically frightened. The thought of revealing his feelings and thoughts left him feeling vulnerable and exposed. He wondered how he would explain his pain and anger. What if he cried—and what if he couldn't stop?

Bill's verbal roadblocks left Janet feeling ignored and ineffective. Until counseling began, they followed this communication pattern.

The communication problems that Janet and Bill had are common when two people must learn to negotiate their self-expression differences under stressful circumstances. Any minor difficulties were exaggerated by Scott's molestation.

Bill was not unusual in being resistant to counseling. He feared exposing personal weakness at a time when he believed family members were looking to him to be strong. His other fear was irrational but normal. He wondered if the therapist would see him as a crazy person who needed medication. Bill was also silently mulling over his other irrational fear: that because Scott was molested by a male, he would prefer men as sexual partners when he was an adult.

Seeking out a stranger for support was an especially scary proposition. Bill used the excuse that participating in couples or family therapy would just provoke more angst for the family as a whole.

DON'T KEEP THINGS SECRET

It's surprising how many parents don't tell other children in the family that their brother or sister has been molested. In wanting to protect them from hurt or alarm, some caregivers go to great lengths to keep the information secret. While keeping things quiet is not uncommon, it is a mistake.

Other children within the family usually know something is wrong. They may worry that something *they* did is upsetting their parents. Even when kids live away from the home, they too need to be informed.

Sometimes parents disclose the abuse to their other children but share only part of the information. That there is no further explanation can produce anxiety in children. For example, imagine hearing through the grapevine that a friend is getting divorced. Your thoughts immediately zero in on what, where, and how questions. The same concern surfaces in your kids when they hear that their sibling has been harmed. They'll want to know if she's okay and how it happened. Small children just need to know that their sibling is okay, but older children need more information.

Furthermore, preventing all your children from participating in therapy is shortchanging them from expressing themselves as well. Although they may not attend every session, they need to be given the opportunity to voice their concerns and have their fears addressed.

Families with communication problems have much to gain by sitting down with an impartial coach. Although child sexual abuse is the reason for counseling, other long-standing conflicts can be resolved. Therapists report that people will often remark to other family members, "I didn't know you felt that way," or "When you ask me in a nice way rather than in a demanding way, I want to give you what you need."

BACK TO THE THOMPSONS

After meeting with members individually and in pairs, Phil saw the Thompson family together. He noted where members sat and who spoke to whom. He also listened to how they spoke with each other. One of his ultimate goals was to witness unguarded discussion about how each member felt about Scott's molestation.

In the family session, Phil asked how he could help. Bill expressed an interest in clearing up any problems as soon as possible so that the family could "get back on track." Janet wanted to be sure there were no long-term problems for Scott as a result of his experience and expressed a desire for family peace. Scott wanted his mom and dad to stop bickering and acting so careful around him. Beth didn't like all the attention paid to Scott. And Brad didn't see why he needed to go to therapy at all.

Phil's job was to create a safe environment for family members to express themselves. He surmised that Janet and Bill were afraid to burden each other and stuck to not getting beyond superficial personal disclosure. He approached their problems as an opportunity to introduce deeper issues.

Scott shyly commented that he didn't want people to think he was being a baby. He looked at his older brother for a response when he continued to say that he thought Brad was cool. He wanted Brad's approval. But he said it bothered him when Brad called him a "faggot" when he was joking around. Brad had no idea his kid brother thought so highly of him. Consequently, he softened a little when Phil suggested the brothers spend more time together.

In following sessions, Phil asked family members to speak directly to one another or rephrase their comments to sound less blameful. For example, when Bill remarked to Janet, "You make me feel guilty when you're on the phone talking to another agency person while I'm relaxing," Phil asked Bill to drop the "you make me" and instead say simply, "I feel guilty." His suggestion sent a message to Bill about taking personal responsibility for his own feelings.

When Beth blurted out, "You don't love me anymore!" to her parents, Phil helped her to say, "I miss being with you." This was a truer comment that helped her parents listen without becoming defensive.

Phil also knew that the message itself isn't what usually turns people off. It's the presentation of the message that makes a difference. He suggested that people use "I" statements and transitional phrases when they wanted to make a point. For instance, Janet was asked to introduce her message by saying, "I don't know if this is something I have mentioned before . . ." instead of, "You didn't hear me when I said this before!" She sent the same message both times, but the presentation was very different. People cannot take in information when they're feeling defensive or under attack. Inviting pre-sentations go further in making a point.

The family's therapist added "homework" between counseling sessions. Janet and Bill were to have a date night each week; special time was to be set for a family activity that wasn't to include playing on the computer, and everyone was asked to notice and stop themselves when they were getting ready to blow off steam in negative ways.

Over the next weeks, the family reported feeling less tension. Janet and Bill began to relax, freeing them to be more emotionally available to their children and to one another. Even Brad admitted to enjoying Sunday dinners. Scott was more spontaneous with his sister, and Beth's stomachaches melted away.

At one especially poignant session, Scott discussed his molestation with his parents. Hesitant at first, Scott answered Janet and Bill's questions after his initial statement. Phil was careful not to push Scott or guide his folks too far with their questions.

During this discussion, both parents were able to demonstrate concern without avoiding sensitive material. They'd had no idea how extensive Mr. Webster's abuse was, and they were able to absorb the amount of pain their son had endured. Janet and Scott were deeply affected by Bill's tenderness and sensitivity, and Janet was able to demonstrate her strength in front of her son. At the conclusion of the session, both parents repeated that they were proud of Scott for his courage and resilience. They again stated that he did nothing to encourage the abuse and they were saddened but not overwhelmed by the information. The session was powerful for everyone.

Phil was impressed by the Thompsons. He knew that they would have continued challenges, but their approach to solving problems was changing. With practice, they were getting better at expressing their needs and feelings. Bill and Janet were beginning to view life from a realistic perspective when it came to their roles and capabilities, and they learned to be a bit easier on themselves. Scott was reassured, and Beth knew she hadn't done anything wrong when it came to the attention being focused in her brother's direction. Brad had become a little more tolerant with his parents, and they, in turn, were able to address his college time lines.

As Bill remarked to Phil, "I was reluctant to come to counseling, but what it's done for our family is great!" Later, every family member was gently reminded by the others to get back on the communication wagon when they lapsed into former negative habits. Even Beth was overheard having a therapy session with her dolls.

The following reality check shares some guidelines for improving family communication.

Reality Check 17: Improving Family Communication

✓ Don't keep your feelings secret. Worrying that you're a burden or that you have no right to say what you think or need contributes to believing that you don't matter. Many times we explode because we feel invisible to other family members. Keeping things quiet supports angry behavior patterns.

✓ Practice what you've learned in counseling. It's easy to fall back into old communication habits simply because they *are* habits. But over time, you'll notice a difference.

✓ Examine your physical markers for tension and anger. When your body is growing more tense and you feel internal heat, stop and ask yourself what's going on. Breathe or drink some cold water as you answer this important personal question.

✓ Report your body tension or anger buildup, and ask for help. In other words, don't let your feelings boil over. Take responsibility for what's happening internally even though you may not have created the problem.

✓ When sharing personal feelings, speak openly without blaming someone else. Shouting, name calling, and sarcasm don't build relationships.

✓ Use a timer during a serious discussion or when negotiating an agreement. At the end of the time (usually five minutes), your partner will use the timer to respond. Timers slow down conversations, help people to be thoughtful, and stop interruptions.

✓ Notice and positively comment on good behavior.

✓ Write loving messages to family members.

✓ Don't guess what the other person is thinking. Ask him or her. We're often stopped from inquiring because we're afraid of what the other person will say. But we can't control everything, so we may as well get our questions out in the open. We might find that the answer is completely different from the one we projected.

✓ Surprise a family member by doing her chores or washing his dishes.

✓ Set aside time to discuss important issues. Make an appointment when you are both free from hunger, exhaustion, and distractions. And so you don't forget what you want to say, write it down.

✓ As much as we wish it, people just can't read our minds. Partners will often say something along the lines of, "She should have known. We've been married a long time!" But the truth is that it's impossible to be 100 percent clairvoyant. Don't expect people to know. Let them know, and you won't be disappointed.

✓ Take a time-out if your anger is getting out of control.

✓ Unless the situation is serious, avoid delivering ultimatums.

✓ If someone needs a time-out, let him take it. Don't follow after him or block the door. Let things cool off.

✓ Be honest, but avoid being blunt. A spoonful of sugar *does* help the medicine go down.

✓ "I'm sorry" is not a four-letter word. Take responsibility for mistakes, and remember that all the saints we know are dead.

✓ Share a joke or riddle every night at the dinner table.

✓ Reward an especially positive discussion by going out for ice cream, renting a funny video, or simply giving each other a hug.

THERAPY: THE RIGHT ANTIDOTE

The Thompsons' experience is not unusual. Initially, they were somewhat nervous about divulging their family secrets to a stranger, and they weren't keen on the idea of expressing their emotions. But with the right therapist, they soon felt comfortable.

Remember that no matter how uncomfortable it may seem to talk with an outsider, the results can mean the difference between getting on with your lives or staying stuck in self-destructive communication patterns.

Therapy isn't rocket science, and it isn't a magical cure. It requires that you put forth effort and work with your therapist in order to acquire renewed meaning in your life. Your entire family's well-being is well worth the time, money, and energy.

13

Dealing with Extended Family and Others

You may wonder what to say to extended family and friends about your child's sexual molestation. If these people live with you or nearby or are otherwise intimately involved with your family, the issue can be confusing.

If the sexual assault receives any newspaper or television coverage, your child's name will not be mentioned, but it's likely that those closest to you will put two and two together. Keep in mind that you do not have to respond to anyone's questions or comments until you've had a chance to gather your thoughts. In any case, it will be left completely to you to decide whom you will tell. And in some instances, such as the other camping parents in Scott's case, there were other people involved already.

At first, Janet and Bill felt they didn't want to share any information about Scott's experience with anyone other than their own kids. Bill was an only child who was dealing with his mother's living transition. Janet's family lived close by, but except for her sister, she was reluctant to disclose to anyone else.

In preparation for the coming holidays, Janet and Bill anticipated that the issue might however come up with extended family members. Consequently, Janet phoned her sister and felt relief when her disclosure about Scott was met with support. Boosted by her sister's response, Janet decided to tell her parents as well.

During a Sunday phone conversation with her mom, Janet approached the subject. She mentioned that Scott's camping leader had behaved inappropriately with him and assured her mother that she and Bill had taken steps to protect their son. Understandably, Janet's mother was shocked and upset. But she let Janet know she would be extra cautious around her grandson. Janet replied that Scott worried people *would* treat him differently, so she gently asked her mom to follow their normal routine.

During the same conversation, her mother asked her not to share the information with Janet's dad because he might voice his opinions during the holiday dinner. She was afraid that after a few drinks, he'd make a scene.

Janet agreed, but later she changed her mind. She informed her mom that she needed her father's support too. So during their father-daughter conversation, she remarked that while she knew his strong feelings on child abuse, his comments would add more stress at the holiday meal. Her dad agreed not to bring up the topic in front of the family. Later, at the family dinner, he managed to control himself. The occasion was festive, undimmed by the shadow of the abuse.

Janet was able to tell close family members without compromising her or her son's integrity. The following reality check shares advice about addressing the abuse with others.

Reality Check 18: What to Keep in Mind When You're Thinking About Talking to Other People

✓ Protecting your child's privacy should be your primary concern.

✓ You don't owe it to anyone to share what happened. If you do share information, keep it superficial unless you're speaking with the authorities or your therapist.

✓ Depending on the age of your child, he has the right to decide whom to tell and know whom you've told about the abuse.

✓ Ask those people you've told to keep the information confidential.

✓ Write down or keep in mind simple responses to people's inquiries or comments. Share them with your child so that he can use them too.

✓ Remember that very young children have primitive communication filters and may share personal information about the abuse at inappropriate moments and in public places.

✓ If you have to be firm, abrupt, or rude in order to protect your child's privacy, it's okay. Your child's well-being comes first.

RESPECTING YOUR CHILD'S FEELINGS

Children often feel embarrassed and ashamed about their sexual assault, so tell only pertinent family or close friends if you must share information.

Sometimes an extended family member is the first person your child tells about the abuse. If this is true for you, understand that your child, for various reasons, probably wanted the safest response to her disclosure. Resist expressing hurt or defensiveness with your child. Don't be upset with the family member because she or he happens to be the messenger of trouble. Chances are this person is close to you too, so your child's decision to share was based on getting the message to you in the best possible way.

In spite of our best intentions to keep certain matters private, unsettling events get discussed in closely knit families. If this is one of your considerations, try to keep in mind how these relatives deal with stress or bad news. The reactions from others can cover a range of behavior: hysteria, obvious distress, sincere concern, embarrassment, horror, disgust, polite indifference, disinterest, or unnecessary probing. If you're already familiar with your mother-in-law's hysterical crying in front of her grandchildren, you may wish to rethink letting her know.

If your relationship with family is long distance or rather cool, it's easier to delay relaying the news or not mention it at all. If for some reason family members need to know, use your support team to help you disclose and shore you up following your disclosure.

RESPONDING TO OTHERS' COMMENTS AND REACTIONS

In some families and communities, news travels fast, so people may approach you even before you've had the opportunity to tell others. Or they may visit or phone to express sympathy or anger before you've had a chance to discuss the situation with authorities.

One mother reported that her daughter's grandparents were so upset after hearing about the child's molestation that they couldn't talk to the child without becoming tearful. The little girl was put in the awkward position of comforting her own grandparents.

People's reactions toward sexual abuse are different and unpredictable. Some family or friends may experience grief similar to your own. Appreciate their concern and continue to set boundaries around your child's privacy. In other instances, people may whisper as they speak about the abuse and exaggerate your child's condition by using phrases such as "that poor thing" or "he's a marked child for sure." Make it clear that while your child suffered a violation, he is not damaged goods.

You cannot be sure that your child's molestation will be kept within the circle of extended family and friends (see Megan's Story on the following page). While Megan's mother chose to withdraw, she could have approached Kathy's parents in a nonconfrontational way and requested they keep the information to themselves. The next reality check shares a few of the infinite variety of comments

---

Megan's Story

Ten year-old Megan shared her abuse with her best friend, Kathy. Kathy told her parents, who began to tell their friends and associates. At a Fourth of July picnic, Megan's mother overheard a stranger refer to Megan as the "dear little Keller girl who was raped." Embarrassed and ashamed, Megan's mom subsequently kept her family away from social events and isolated themselves from their group of friends.

---

that well-meaning family and acquaintances may say to you. Being forewarned about the possibility of such insensitive remarks will help you be prepared.

Reality Check 19: What Others May Say

"Don't you just want to kill that perp?"

"How did you ever get your child in that situation?"

"Where were you when your child was molested?"

"Couldn't you see it coming?"

"Why didn't you know it was happening?"

"If it were my child, I'd move away."

"Your child doesn't need therapy."

"Kids forget about these things. Take him to Disney World."

"What exactly did he do to your child?"

"Haven't you filed a lawsuit yet?"

"I don't know how you can live with yourself."

"Your child may never get over this."

"For Pete's sake, don't let the police know!"

"Didn't you check that school out?"

"Whatever you do, don't let them put him on any type of medication."

SPECIAL CONSIDERATIONS WITH REGARD TO INCEST

In cases of incest, don't become defensive if you hear first about the assault from a family member or friend. People who have been told first by a child are put in an awful position. Be sure to ask your family or friend messenger if she or he has shared the information with other people and request that they not inform anyone else unless it's the authorities.

Many families have been split apart because adults or children have been unsupportive of the child victim when there has been incest. Denial is often present, and some members deliver ultimatums and cease further contact with one another.

YOU DON'T OWE ANYONE AN EXPLANATION!

"I'm not willing to discuss it" can stop an inquisitive relative or acquaintance from asking about the abuse. Another generic response is, "I appreciate your concern," accompanied by a nod of acknowledgment.

Unless you trust your listener to be discreet, don't share information about your child's abuse. Remember that you don't have to say anything if you don't care to share. But if you want to use questions as opportunities to educate those who ask, you can speak generally about the effects of child sexual abuse and what you've learned from your experience. You can emphasize the importance of reporting and early therapy intervention. For example, in response to an insensitive comment, such as, "Don't you feel guilty?" you can say that all parents with a sexually molested child go through a grief process that includes guilt.

Being asked why you weren't there to stop the abuse can push your buttons, but you don't have to respond to unkind or thoughtless comments. You don't have to answer directly or at all, especially when people press you for details.

HELPING YOUR CHILD
WHEN HE'S QUESTIONED

Adults are the ones who are most likely to ask your child questions. Unless they're with the investigation team or your therapist, you can direct your child to decline answering. Arm him with some simple responses—for example:

"My parents told me I don't have to talk about it."

"I don't want to talk about it."

"I'm not ready to say anything."

"I'm a pretty strong person."

"I have people I can talk to, but thanks anyway."

"Some things we have to work out with experts."

"This has happened to other people, and they got through it."

Some children feel comfortable talking to anybody. Young children in particular may want to tell the mail carrier, grocery check-out lady, or any other smiling person. If you think he is talking about the molestation inappropriately, let him know in a calm, loving way that he can discuss or talk about it with certain people, such as Mommy, Daddy, Granny, his brother, or a close adult friend. Ask him to speak about it when he is at his house or their houses, but not in stores where people buy things or when the mail carrier delivers letters.

Even if your child's comments seem off-base, don't react strongly. Simply redirect his discussion or distract him in some other way. You don't need to say a word to any of the people he disclosed to. Just smile, and change the subject.

Counseling will serve as a support while you deal with any former ideas about owing someone an answer when you're asked a question about the assault. Meanwhile, having answers ready will help you feel in control when the sexual abuse subject is broached by unwelcome questioners.

REASSURING NEWS

If there is no fuel to flame a fire, it will die fairly quickly. This analogy applies to your child's sexual assault as well. If not fed information, people will generally stop their questions and lose interest. Be comforted by the fact that their interrogations reflect a temporary situation. As time passes, the molestation will become less of a topic of conversation or a central issue to family and acquaintances.

The next chapter offers tips for preparing and supporting your child throughout the court process.

14

When You or Your Child
Must Appear in Court

Your child's case may never go to trial, but in the event it becomes necessary for her to appear in court, this chapter offers information on what to expect and how to prepare.

The preliminary hearing or a grand jury hearing could be your child's first court appearance. If either of these proceedings determines that there is probable cause to prosecute the alleged perpetrator, an indictment will follow and a criminal trial date will be set. (You will not make the decision if the defendant will be prosecuted by the state. Remember that these cases reflect criminal action.)

The prosecutor's office may request a grand jury to review the evidence of a criminal act. Witnesses are called to testify before the grand jury and are subject to questioning by a prosecuting attorney and grand jurors. In a grand jury proceeding, the defendant and his attorney do not participate in the proceeding and are not present.

In some situations and jurisdictions, a defendant has the right to an adversary preliminary hearing based on the charges pending against him. A preliminary hearing is essentially a minitrial, held with a presiding judge and defendant present. Witnesses are called to testify and are subject to cross-examination by the defense attorney. The burden of the state is to convince a judge to set the matter over for trial.

PREPARING FOR COURT

Knowing what to expect is the best way to prepare you and your child if the criminal case goes to trial. The process will seem less overwhelming and frightening to your child when you both have an idea about the legal process leading up to the trial, as well as the courtroom proceedings.

The proceedings can stir up old feelings, especially if you've worked hard to address them in therapy. You may feel that your life has been disrupted all over again just as things were getting back to normal. And you may be surprised that your initial punitive stance toward the molester may have mellowed into just wanting to put the ordeal to rest. You may also resent the fact that once again your time and energies are being focused on your child's assault.

Be sure to discuss your feelings in counseling or with other supportive people. If you are no longer in therapy, you may want to give your therapist a call and schedule a session for you and perhaps for your child as well.

You can be psychologically strengthened by knowing about depositions and videotaped testimony.

Depositions

A *deposition* is a recorded sworn statement usually delivered at an attorney's office. If your child must give a deposition, have the prosecutor explain the procedure. Usually individuals can be deposed, or questioned, only once unless new evidence is turned up between the deposition and trial.

In additional to the defense and prosecuting attorneys, a court reporter, your child, a victim advocate such as a guardian ad litem, and perhaps you will be present at the deposition. (A guardian ad litem is a volunteer or professional person assigned by the court to protect and make recommendations that are in the interest of the child.) The defense attorney usually has the right to decide whether to allow the parent or caregiver to sit in.

Defense attorneys have historically been resistant to taking child depositions, and the prosecutor may use this as a bargaining tool. If the alleged perpetrator is maintaining innocence, the prosecuting attorney may insist that all other depositions be taken before your child's, thus making it clear that the state will not be as open to plea bargaining after your child has been deposed. This type of strategy can prompt a more favorable response from the defense.

Videotaped Testimony

If your child can handle testifying in person, she will probably be asked to do so. The emotional impact on a jury is usually stronger when children appear in person. In addition, children may feel relief and empowered when they take an active role in challenging their assailant. If an appearance in court will retraumatize a child and it is legally allowable, the prosecuting attorney may ask the judge's permission to use taped testimony.

Whether your child will testify in person or through videotape is often decided after court proceedings begin. The judge and the defense and prosecuting attorneys follow the same court procedure if a videotape is deemed necessary. Parents may not be allowed in the room or in sight of the child during the taped interviews.

YOUR CHILD'S COURT APPEARANCE

The prospect of appearing in court can seem frightening or overwhelming to you or your child (or both of you). But with proper preparation, it should carry no long-term ill effects for anyone. When you and your child know what to expect, the process becomes less intimidating.

An identified victim advocate such as your prosecuting attorney, child protection team worker, or court volunteer will prepare you for court. Understandably, you will wish to walk through the orientation process with your child when it comes time to visit a courtroom and become educated about giving testimony. In some areas, discussion or a videotaped explanation will take the place of a courtroom visit. And if none of your support team has mentioned anything about an orientation meeting close to your trial date, be sure and ask when you and your child will be informed.

The following reality check discusses how to prepare children for their court appearance. Write down any other questions you have, and ask one of your support team members to address them prior to trial.

Reality Check 20: Preparing Your Child to Appear in Court

✓ A courtroom can intimidate even secure adults. Think carefully about how your child is likely to be affected when she walks into the room and speaks in front of the alleged perpetrator.

✓ Be sure your child understands that the person who will be on trial is the alleged molester, not her. Because your child may hear the upcoming court appearance described as "your trial," be sure to explain that a trial doesn't judge *her*. She is not being questioned to find out if she did something wrong. She is being questioned because people want her to tell the truth about what happened. Let her know that a trial is the way our society finds out if people are guilty or not guilty. But she is not guilty of anything.

✓ Ask your child the following questions:

What does she think about appearing in court?

What does she think that judges do?

What does she think about talking in front of strangers?

What does she imagine the courthouse, the courtroom, the lawyers, and the judge look like?

Does she have any fears or worries? If she does, let her know that the alleged perpetrator will not try to harm her. A man called a bailiff is there to protect her.

How you can help her feel comfortable? Is there anything she wants to carry into the courtroom? Would she like to eat something special for breakfast the morning of the trial? Does she want a close relation such as her grandmother to sit in the courtroom? How does she want your support?

Really listen to your child's answers to these questions. Be careful not to interrupt before giving reassuring feedback. Let her finish, and then clarify any misperceptions she may have about the court appearance process and any of the people who will be involved. Make sure she understands what you are saying by pausing often and checking to see if she has been able to digest the information you are providing.

✓ Few of us have much experience with the legal system. If you find your own knowledge has serious gaps, don't hesitate to ask one of your support team members for help.

✓ It will help your child tremendously to visit a courtroom before the trial with one of her victim advocates. You will more than likely visit an empty courtroom, but in the rare case that court is in process, quietly enter the room and speak softly. Make sure your child knows that none of the same people, except maybe the judge, will be present when she appears in court. If possible when taking the courtroom tour, let your child sit on the judge's bench or chair, in the jury box, on the witness chair, and anywhere else she wishes. This exercise will help her get a sense of the environment and have a picture in mind when she thinks about the upcoming trial.

✓ Explain that a court reporter will be there to record what everyone says so that there is a written record. The court reporter speaks when he or she wants to confirm what was said and keeps things confidential.

✓ Be sure your child meets the attorney who will be presenting the case in court. Ideally, it will be the same person who has been involved in the criminal case from the beginning, but if it isn't, your child should meet the new person *before* the trial day.

✓ The prosecuting attorney should go over the questions she will be asking your child when she takes the stand. This is not rehearsing the witness. It is a proper way of preparing, so don't let this make you uncomfortable. Attorneys who fail to prepare their witnesses properly are being negligent in their professional duties.

✓ You should be prepared to hear the defense either insinuate or say outright that your child is lying. Let your child know that the attorney who will be defending the alleged perpetrator may try to trick her or suggest to her while she is testifying that she is not telling the truth. You can explain that sometimes defense attorneys can be confusing when they ask questions like, "You were told to say these things, weren't you?" or "That didn't really happen, did it?" Reassure her that you and her helpers know she is telling the truth. Let her know that when she doesn't understand questions, she can ask people to explain themselves more clearly by saying, "I don't understand." Because people don't want to go to jail, they'll sometimes lie. So continue to explain that trying to make her look bad is one of the plans defense attorneys use all the time.

Whatever is said to your child is not about her. It's not personal.

Remember that a common tactic is to discredit the witness, even if the witness is only five years old. A young child may not know the time of year or the day of the week when an incident occurred, particularly when the trial is taking place much later. An age-appropriate lack of detail in a child's testimony can be presented as unreliable by the defense to the judge or jury.

✓ Let your child know if the defense attorney who questioned her at the deposition is the same one who will be speaking to her in court.

✓ Explain where everyone will be seated in court, including the alleged perpetrator.

✓ Your child should be made aware of the questions she will be asked to answer and should understand that if she doesn't know an answer, she doesn't have to make one up. Reassure her that she can always say, "I don't know" or "I don't remember."

✓ Stress to your child that when she takes the oath to tell the truth, she must not exaggerate or make anything up. She must tell the truth.

✓ Let your child know in advance if any pictures or anatomically correct dolls will be used for demonstration in court.

✓ Tell your child that you cannot predict or control what
   the defense attorney will say.

✓ Let your child know that the outcome of the trial is
   not her responsibility and that sometimes the final
   decision may not seem fair.

✓ Let your child know that at a trial, a judge may decide
   the outcome or a jury may decide the outcome,
   depending on if it's a bench or jury trial.

✓ Children can view their original videotaped interview
   before the trial in order to refresh their memory.
   This visual review helps them remember the sexual
   assault. Your child will need one of the support team
   members to sit with her while she reviews the tape to
   guide her through the experience.

WHEN YOU'RE CALLED AS A WITNESS

If you're going to be called as a witness during a trial, you may or
may not be allowed in the courtroom until it's time for your testimony. Your child should know ahead of time if you will not be there
during her testimony. And if a child protection advocacy member
is testifying, he or she should provide another familiar person to sit
in the courtroom while your child is testifying.

   If it's too emotionally overwhelming, you may choose not to be
in the courtroom. Because trials don't immediately follow your abuse
report, you may have already worked through overpowering feelings.

   Appearances make a lasting impression in court, so dress con-
servatively. A black or navy blue suit sends the message that you are
serious. Never dress in a casual manner, and cover as many body
parts as possible. If your hair normally hangs down, tie it back.

   Remember that appearing as a witness is simply swearing to tell
the truth and answering questions. The experience can be intimi-

dating, but remember to answer the questions simply. Don't elaborate, and when it's possible, answer yes or no. If you don't understand a question, say, "I don't understand." If you don't know an answer, say, "I don't know." And if you don't remember, say, "I don't remember."

Keep your emotions in check, but don't become a robot either. The jury or judge will be interested to see if you've been affected by your child's sexual abuse.

The defense attorney may want you to show your temper and demonstrate out-of-control behavior. Hold your tongue if he insinuates you coached a disclosure out of your child or that she lied. He may lead up to a final question by asking you if your child has ever lied and then add that since she's lied in the past, she could be lying now. *Don't let these comments rattle you. They are part of the defense strategy.*

You may become emotionally prepared to go to trial and then have it postponed. This can happen more than once.

WHEN THE VERDICT IS "NOT GUILTY"

If the alleged perpetrator was found not guilty in a criminal trial, it doesn't necessarily mean he isn't guilty, and it doesn't discredit your child's testimony. It simply means the molester was found not legally guilty. Be sure your child understands so that she doesn't take responsibility for the decision. Other family members need to be informed as well.

A not guilty verdict may be easier to understand if you realize that child sexual abuse can be a difficult crime for investigators and prosecutors to process. There is not a usual crime scene because most sexual abuse crimes are nonviolent, involving no forceful physical contact. And unless there are or were visible physical indications of the abuse, there is usually no evidence.

Most sexual abuse crimes are not witnessed, so the trial is based on one-on-one testimony. In other words, it's the child's word against the alleged perpetrator's. Juries must decide whether a child's disclosure is true. Often the older defendant appears more articulate and surer. Although child protective service professionals may support her allegations, it's not unusual for juries to determine that a child misunderstood what happened.

Understandably, juries and judges are more comfortable when there are witnesses, evidence, and a crime scene. And because the alleged perpetrator is usually well groomed for the trial and looks like anyone else, it confuses people. One child advocacy worker remarked that if she didn't know better, she might be one of those jury members who would find it difficult to accept the testimony of a five year old. Considering the consequences that often include a prison term, the responsibility is daunting for jurors and judges.

If the alleged perpetrator is found not guilty, try to avoid letting your child witness any great gestures of defeat or despair. Try to praise your child for doing something you knew was difficult. And tell her that what she did was extremely important and that something positive was accomplished. She is not about to let anyone hurt her!

Fortunately, public awareness is growing about child sexual abuse. As a result, child disclosures are seriously considered, and sex offender treatment is also viewed as an important part of sentencing.

THE OUTCOME FOR SCOTT

Scott was nervous the day he testified. He was reassured, however, by the presence of his camping buddies. They sat together drinking sodas and playing with their video games while they waited to testify.

There was a mixture of triumph and sadness when Mr. Webster was found guilty and later sentenced to prison. The Thompsons and other families felt that justice had been served, yet they were sad that so many children had been affected by a terrible experience.

Scott Thompson's reaction was relief. He was happy not to talk to any more adults about the abuse unless it was *his* choice. Phil, his therapist, thought that Scott had grieved his experience to the extent that a nine year old grieves. He knew that Scott might return to therapy later for a brief time, especially when he was growing through another developmental stage such as puberty. Phil was on hand to support Scott during the trial, and he was impressed by the boy's confidence.

Janet and Bill were pleased about the trial outcome as well. They felt that Mr. Webster's sexual perversion had been disrupted, and they were happy they had made a report. They echoed one another when they stated that family therapy was the most positive aspect of the whole experience.

Mr. Webster's sentence was a resolution to the months of anxiety building up to the trial. The family was free to pursue more engaging activities as they resumed normal living.

15

When the Sexual Abuse Is Incest

I f your child's sexual abuser is a legal, social, or biological family member, there are additional and more complex problems. These issues can potentially destroy your child's caring relationships and his trust.

The wide variety of living arrangements today has contributed to broadening the definition of incest. Perpetrators of incest have been expanded to include nonblood relatives who are related by marriage or have assumed family member roles. The following examples would be classified as incestuous relationships by most child abuse experts:

> GRAMPA JOE. "Grampa Joe" had taken a special lik-
> ing to his step-grandson, Pete, and frequently invited
> Pete to stay at his house. One day, the seven year old
> reported to his parents that his grandfather had been
> rubbing the child's penis at bedtime, explaining it as a
> way to help the boy fall asleep.

> EDDIE AND SARA. Eddie's mom married Sara's dad
> two years ago, and they became a blended family. Later
> that year, when Sara was three, eleven-year-old Eddie
> began taking her into a bedroom closet and molesting
> her. One day, his older brother opened the closet door

and found Eddie lying on top of Sara, their underwear pulled down around their ankles.

ANDREW AND HIS MOM. Andrew's mom had been divorced a while. Without many friends, she was especially close to her ten-year-old son, but her behavior seriously blurred parent-child boundaries. Andrew reported that she often invited him to sleep in the same bed and routinely asked him to rub her naked back with lotion. Struggling with arthritis, she had also asked him to remove her underwear and stockings as well.

UNCLE MIKE AND AUNT DORKAS. Aunt Dorkas strongly defended her husband, Mike, when he was caught fondling their eight-year-old niece while she sat on his lap. She didn't understand why the family had a problem. As she explained her husband's behavior, "He loves his nieces and nephews and wouldn't do a thing to harm them. People don't understand his affectionate ways. Never did."

IF YOU WERE MOLESTED EARLIER BY A RELATIVE

It's not unusual for a relative who has molested you to attempt to molest your child. Because child sex offenders seldom change their sexual arousal patterns, they will repeat behaviors. Don't assume that just because the person is older, he or she is now "safe."

Just as sexual abuse does not have to include sexual intercourse in order to be identified as sexual assault, the person who molested you may have tried to persuade you or others that there was no incest because "only light touch occurred." Don't believe it, and don't assume your former molester will behave differently with your child!

YOUR RESPONSE

If your child has been molested by your spouse or anyone else with whom you've had a sexual relationship, you have a responsibility as your child's protector to:

- Report the sexual assault to your local child abuse hot line.

- Demand, at the very least, a temporary end to all contact and visitations between the alleged perpetrator and your child.

- Obtain the necessary court orders to enforce your demands.

- Accept nothing short of complete protection for your child.

- Express anger in appropriate ways. And don't force yourself to smooth over the situation, especially when the child sex offender offers an apology in exchange for secrecy.

The child sex offender must leave your home. If she or he has not been living there, visits or contact with your child should be stopped immediately. In most states, nonoffending parents don't have a choice whether the alleged perpetrator leaves the home: it is mandatory.

If the alleged perpetrator stays, there is a likelihood that your child will be removed and placed with relatives or in another protective setting. If this happens, a child protective service professional will regularly visit your child and you will have supervised visitation for a time.

Even when a decision is made not to pursue criminal charges, a social service agency may still remain involved when there is concern for your child's safety. The state can petition for temporary custody and provide child protective supervision for a period of time.

WHEN YOUR CHILD IS
REMOVED FROM HOME

Try to imagine your child's experience if he were to be removed from his home. He is away from familiar touchstones and exposed to strange routines. He may have to attend a different school and adjust to different methods of discipline. His friends and close relations may not be accessible. And most of all, he is separated from you. All of these circumstances can create additional trauma.

If your child is placed with other children, he may hear horror stories and be exposed to their disruptive or aggressive behaviors. Children often obsess about where they'll end up living and fear being placed permanently away from their family. These kids are in the terrible position of not knowing what the next day holds, and they can imagine the worst. During these stressful times, they may recant their disclosures, hoping they'll be returned home. Changed stories usually don't change their living arrangements, however, and often reflect Child Abuse Accommodation Syndrome mentioned earlier in the book.

WHEN PARENTS BLAME THEIR CHILD

You're adding to your child's trauma if you blame him. He will feel frightened and abandoned, contributing to his acquiring psychological problems and abnormal behaviors.

Sometimes the nonoffending parent's loyalties are torn, especially if the child has misbehaved or has otherwise been difficult to live with. And sometimes the molester has been the only disciplinarian. His absence could mean you will be taking on additional responsibilities and stress.

More than one parent has envisioned a bleak future without the financial support of the jailed child sex offender. When believing and protecting a child is associated with devastating consequences, parents may begin to rationalize child sex offender behaviors and subtly suggest that the child recant his disclosures. This serves to further confuse children, who need their parents' assurances.

One therapist recounted an experience she had several years ago with one mother named Pam and her daughter, Monique.

Pam and Monique's Story

Pam's common-law husband, Craig, was not Monique's birth father, but they had lived together since the child was three years old.

In first grade, Monique was intrigued by the special child abuse prevention program presented for her class. The program described "good touch, bad touch." The little girl felt as though she had made a big discovery when she told her teacher that her "daddy" touched her in her "privates" on more than one occasion. She asked the teacher, "Is that bad?"

When her teacher reported the disclosure, Pam was upset and believed that Craig had been falsely accused of touching Monique. No amount of physical evidence, education, or advisement by professionals would convince her that he had done anything wrong. "Kids get these things from toilets" or "Monique doesn't know what she's saying" were her usual responses. When the investigators said that either Craig or Monique needed to leave the home, Pam's high blood pressure skyrocketed.

> Her doctor put her in the hospital, and Monique
> was placed with her mother's sister.
>
> During the crisis, Craig left town and headed for
> Mexico. While he was gone, Pam and Monique
> were court-ordered into counseling. Several months
> later, Craig returned without the authorities'
> knowledge. Pam demonstrated little insight when
> she called her therapist and asked that the entire
> family be seen for counseling but that the counselor
> keep Craig's reappearance a secret.

ADDITIONAL PRESSURES

Pressures bear down hard on families when incest has occurred. When a stepfather has been reported, the mother of the child victim may blame herself to the extent that she pressures herself into taking on more responsibility for the assault than the perpetrator. "If I had paid more attention to him, he wouldn't have tried anything with my child" is a comment some women voice. Be assured that *no one except the child molester* is responsible for molesting a child or youth.

Remember that a child may have good feelings about his molester because part of their relationship may have been nurturing. When a caring relationship goes beyond acceptable boundaries, it must be interrupted. Nevertheless, it can be heart wrenching to witness your child's distress if he doesn't understand why the person who molested him must stay away.

Pressure by other family members not to report the assault to the authorities can be powerful. It's common for family members to threaten or coerce parents by ceasing contact or lying to authorities. Or they'll blame the child or youth victim. They may even go so far as to hide the sex offender or financially support his defense.

These actions can be heartbreaking. Incest is more complicated when the perpetrator is a family member and people are less ambivalent when the assailant is a stranger.

Keeping your child's protection the number one priority will get you through difficult times. Be sure to ask for help from supportive friends and other relatives when the going gets tough. And remember not to expose your child to family doubters. You may wish to curb your own contact with them as well.

Pressure can even be exerted by well-meaning community or spiritual "helpers." Although they're sincerely offering help, they have not received training in the sexual abuse arena. They aren't experts. One father was told by his clergyman that the family needed to pray about his son's sexual assault by a female member of the congregation instead of reporting it to the authorities.

The pressure that you may feel from the child's assailant can be very difficult, especially when he is romantically tied to you. It would be unnatural if you weren't affected by his arrest or calls from jail.

These circumstances can lead you to feel confused and disoriented for quite a while. If you have feelings for this person, you will grieve the disappointment of your hopes along with your child's personal experience.

Take time to sort things out, and don't place yourself under pressure to move too quickly through your grieving by getting overly busy or caught up in your child's case. Rely on your counselor to guide you through this process, and seek support from other reliable people.

WHEN YOUR CHILD
BECOMES PREGNANT

Cases in which girls have been impregnated by a family member are exceptionally heart-wrenching because youth are confronted with making dramatic decisions. Should they abort the fetus or bring it through to a full-term pregnancy? More often than not, girls will not be aware of their pregnancy until it is too late to make that decision. Often in these situations, their babies will be raised by someone else.

Shame frequently compels these young mothers to keep the birth father's name a secret. Many drug and rehabilitation counselors have heard sad stories shared by recovering women who were sexually abused by family and forced to disown their children.

If these circumstances are true for you, you must stand by your daughter and report her sexual assailant, even if he is married to you. *You must not abandon your child.* You have no choice. Work with a counselor to make any decisions that will affect her future as a mother as well as any that affect your grandchild.

Don't make excuses for the perpetrator either. He may be a cousin, son, half-sibling, spouse, or uncle. You must report him to the authorities.

A social worker shared the following tragic story.

Shawn's Story

I met Shawn twenty-five years ago when she was eleven years old. I was taking her to have an abortion. I had arranged with her grandmother to meet the child one spring morning on her street corner. No one was with her. Not her mother, sister, father . . . nobody. Arrangements had been made earlier by her "grannie," because the old woman felt that Shawn's body was too small to carry and give birth to a baby. Looking at Shawn, I agreed. Had she not had the pregnancy test, I would have thought she still hadn't gotten her period.

Shawn was a little girl, and she talked about little girl things on the way to the abortion clinic.

When we arrived, she walked happily into the orientation office, where we sat to receive information. She was almost giddy because there were
probably rare occasions when she was the center of
attention.

Shawn didn't know which of her three brothers
had planted his sperm. She seemed to be oblivious
even though I tried hard to draw her out in my
attempts to help her grieve or just feel *something*.

After the procedure, we left, and I drove her to
a diner for some ice cream. She liked strawberry.
Late that afternoon, I dropped her off at her house
and insisted on walking inside with her. No one
was home.

TAKING RESPONSIBILITY

As difficult as it may be, nonoffending parents must be willing to
examine how their behaviors may have contributed to the sexual
abuse. While many nonoffending parents report being completely
unaware of what was happening, clues may have been present.
Some clues include the perpetrator's focus on the victim by overly
controlling his behavior and isolating him from friends or other
family members. Not paying attention or otherwise ignoring these
behaviors is negligence.

Other conditions that expose your child to vulnerable situations
include a parent's unavailability for any number of reasons during
crucial hours of the day such as bedtime or wake-up, being unable
to share other caretaking responsibilities, or being inaccessible by
phone or transportation.

Coming to terms with our caregiving blind spots can be especially painful and lead nonoffending parents to rationalize their own

behavior in order to avoid seeing themselves in a less than perfect light. Caregivers should not avoid confronting their parenting gaps that may have left their children vulnerable to sexual assault.

As one parent explained, "The pain of what I experienced was indescribable. When I first heard that my husband had sexually molested our little girl, I was devastated. I know I didn't cause the incest to occur, but I do know that my working nights and sleeping days didn't help the situation either. I was always too tired to spend time with my daughter. I was always in a hurry and didn't want to give up a good-paying job."

WHEN YOU CAN'T FORGIVE YOUR CHILD'S SEXUAL ASSAILANT

You may feel that you can never forgive the person who sexually molested your child. Yet the experience may be additionally devastating for your child if he cannot see his parent even when the parent admits to the offense and works diligently to repair the damage. If the sex offender admits his guilt and accepts full responsibility with genuine remorse, your child's relationship with the perpetrator can be mended over time with appropriate intervention. This doesn't mean that you have to accept the person back in your own life, however.

When nonoffending relatives can't forgive the sex offender, they shouldn't be too hard on themselves. They can fall into exposing themselves and their children to additional abuse if they forgive the child's molester too quickly. Forgiveness is a personal experience. Don't let other people, including family, pressure you into letting bygones be bygones.

You may be able to resume a relationship with the offender or at least forgive him in time. But remember that forgiveness does not mean that boundaries should be loosened or that frank discussions regarding the sexual assault should be avoided.

WHEN INCEST IS DEALT WITH THROUGH SEX OFFENDER PROGRAMS

Successful completion of court-ordered community sex offender treatment is more likely in cases where the assailant has been determined appropriate for community treatment by a qualified evaluator.

Many judges feel that while incest may not be the perpetrator's only sexual deviation, progressive community-based treatment may be more effective than prison. People who are determined competent to proceed through nonprison programs must demonstrate remorse and restitution, have no history of prior offenses, and be placed on probation or on parole.

Counseling through sexual abuse treatment programs becomes another opportunity for nonoffending parents and child victims to work through their recovery and determine their willingness to heal relationships and possibly reunite as a family. These programs are long term, and attendance is court ordered.

"When they told me therapy would last at least twelve months and possibly longer, I wondered why it had to take so long. I didn't think our family had that much to talk about," said one nonoffending parent. "I just thought the system wanted to punish us. It took a long time for my husband and me to see that therapy was our only chance to make things different. We were involved for over three years, and it changed our lives."

An incest victim explains, "I didn't want to say anything to the counselor. I figured I'd created too many problems already. My parents split up, and my mom resented me for a while. But I learned that I hadn't done anything wrong. And I felt good when she was confronted in therapy."

An adjudicated offender reports, "After I got out of prison, I wanted to be with my family. It was impossible unless I went to court-ordered therapy. In retrospect, I think I was trying to avoid taking responsibility for the pain I caused by saying I was sorry. Sure I was sorry, but until I was challenged by my peers and family, I didn't understand how much pain I'd caused. I'm still really self-centered, but I'm working at it, and everybody reports that I seem less selfish and impulsive. Every time I came up with an answer in our sessions, my therapist would have another question. I've learned how my early childhood kind of set up my sexual arousal patterns, and I'm doing a lot of relapse-prevention work too. The antianxiety medication helps as well."

CUSTODY OR VISITATION ALLEGATIONS

If the charges of child sexual abuse against your spouse are part of a divorce, custody, or visitation dispute, you may face special prejudices, even among professionals. This bias can be so strong that in spite of strong evidence indicating there had been sexual abuse during the marriage, the investigation agency may dismiss your claims. They may minimize the circumstances because "this is a custody dispute" or they assume you want to punish your former spouse.

If your lawyer is pressuring you to make compromises because she believes your case will be difficult to prove, keep your child's welfare in mind. How capable is he of protecting himself? What is his relationship with you? The legal compromise is binding.

Your attorney may further explain that even if you bring in an expert witness to substantiate your claim, the witness may be viewed as a hired gun who sells his or her opinions. Your former spouse can also hire an expert to disclaim his claims.

These situations can extend the life of your court case, deplete you of funds, and never really settle the sexual abuse issue. Be prepared to spend time in counseling so that you don't transfer your feelings toward your children. And stick with the case if you fear your child's safety is in jeopardy.

DEALING WITH INCEST

It takes great courage on your part to bring your child's incest to light. To say that the process is brief and simple would be misleading. Incest is the most gruesome betrayal. It betrays your child's innocence and trust, and it creates secrets that have long-term consequences. Rely on your inner strength, and use your support system as you work to protect your child and hold the perpetrator accountable. Monsters don't live in the light.

16

You Know Your Family
Is Getting Better When . . .

A year had passed since Scott had made his disclosure to his dad. As Janet and Bill relaxed over coffee one night, they discussed their family's experience. It had been a long year, and they had been introduced to several less appealing aspects of life. This introduction was sudden and extremely challenging.

Before Scott's disclosure, Janet and Bill had never given much thought to their community's human service agencies or the judicial system. They assumed that detectives, child welfare workers, and psychotherapists were there mainly to help other people—people less fortunate than they. But the sexual assault forced them to look closely at their presumptions as well as the effectiveness of the child protection and court systems.

In addition, both parents had been naive about the lengthiness of the legal process. They had imagined Scott's perpetrator arrested and jailed immediately after they made the child abuse hot line report. They had assumed the investigation and trial would move quickly because Webster's guilt seemed so apparent.

Had it not been for counseling, they may not have handled the situation well. They might have struggled with their unspoken feelings without articulating their needs or clarifying their intentions with one another. Without treatment, Scott would not have dumped his experience in the therapy room or been reassured about his fears. And the entire family may not have renewed their bonds.

A lot of what they learned in counseling was good sense. But had it not been for structured coaching, the Thompsons, who were overcome with stress, might not have made commonsense decisions because they were in crisis.

Bill and Janet remembered their last family session with Phil. He asked them how they were spending time together and wondered if their sessions had been helpful. In response, the family members reflected on their personal changes and how the changes had affected the family as a whole.

For Janet, family counseling had been very positive. She felt a lot of relief about the outcome of the trial, and she felt more connected to her husband and children. Bill, ever the cautious person, quietly commented that his kids were getting along better and he felt more comfortable sharing his feelings with Janet. Scott responded that he felt a lot more relaxed and easygoing. Brad said he learned that the abuse wasn't his brother's fault and not every authority figure has a young person's best interest in mind. Beth said she was much happier because her parents were happier.

Many of the positive changes Janet and Bill reported are reflected in the following reality check. They identify feelings and behaviors that can progress in a positive direction between the sexual abuse disclosure and court resolution. Notice that this list doesn't include forgetting about the assault. A more realistic outcome is that the abuse becomes part of your personal history without the emotional associations.

Reality Check 21: How You Know When Your Family Is Better

✓ Your child's acute or posttraumatic stress symptoms have diminished or disappeared.

✓ Obsessive child or parent thoughts about the sexual assault have been curbed or have ceased.

✓ Your family is less socially isolated.

✓ There is clearer and less blameful family communication.

✓ Your family has resumed its normal routines.

✓ Your child who has been sexually molested behaves in age-appropriate ways. For instance, your eight year old plays with same-age friends rather than engaging with older children of the opposite sex. Or your teenager is no longer using alcohol or drugs to numb her pain. Instead, she's active in sports and dating.

✓ You spend more time with your life partner.

✓ You consider all your children equally.

✓ You spend more time on activities that are fun than writing letters of complaint.

✓ You aren't triggered into rage when you think of your child's sexual perpetrator.

✓ Your sexual relationship with your partner has improved.

✓ You've established family time through regular family dinners, weekend sports, board game contests, and other connection-building activities.

✓ You have discussed a safety plan with each child as it pertains to possible assault scenarios.

✓ You are reasonably cautious but not overly protective with your children.

✓ You are practicing stress-reduction techniques and may be enjoying a new hobby.

✓ You feel less burdened and more empowered.

Building a Safety Plan

- Repeat safety discussions with young children at least every six months. Older children and youth will remember with fewer conversations.

- Discuss a plan of action if your child is approached by a stranger. Let her know that she can call for help and make a fuss if someone becomes bothersome or even appears scary. She can kick, scream, or run away.

- Let her know she has a right to say no to anyone when it pertains to touch. Let her know that her body belongs to her alone, not to anyone else. If someone appears offended when she says no, let her know it doesn't matter what that other person thinks. Children and youth are true innocents and strive to please. In child sexual abuse, this quality has been used against them.

- Let children know they should call you if they're not feeling comfortable in any setting. And above all, don't contribute to their vulnerability by asking them to walk home alone at night or leave them alone with strangers. Remember to do a background check on any potential adult baby-sitters as well as your day care center.

- Get to know your teenager's friends and family. Check out her party sites and potential dates. If your child is dating one person, assume the role of an old-fashioned parent and interview him. Drive home the message that you are fiercely protective of your child.

- If you're a single parent, don't bring any dating part-ners home to meet your children until you have checked them out over a period of time. Let the person know that your children come first. If you're feeling a little wary, feel free to get a background check via law enforcement or private investigation.

- Keep the lines of communication open. These lines stay clear simply by taking time to be with your child. Time spent with children is the best prevention against child sexual assault.

- Many excellent books discuss child safety. Browse through your library or bookstores for selections.

FACTORS THAT CONTRIBUTE TO YOUR RECOVERY

Your family's recovery time depends on a number of factors. Much of them have to do with your history before your child disclosed her sexual molestation. Optimistic and resilient people have a tendency to get on with their healing more easily than those who are depressed or have been troubled by other challenges in the past. There are reasons that people aren't able to recover as quickly; they include chronic illnesses, unemployment, lack of support systems, extended caregiving, addictions, and ineffective or negligent parenting.

If the child molester was a family member, the abuse extended over a long period, or the perpetrator denies the allegations, the legal and recovery process can be slowed down. Obviously a person who admits guilt and expresses remorse will help speed your family's recovery time because the outcome is so clear and freer of legal hurdles.

If the alleged perpetrator was found not guilty, you may spend more time in counseling to come to terms with the jury's or judge's decision. If the alleged perpetrator was not even prosecuted, you may experience a good deal of anger and wonder how you'll ever get beyond this episode.

Janet and Bill Thompson were grateful they took a healthy risk by seeking family therapy. In addition to the other benefits, their children were reassured that their parents would do everything they could to protect them. Scott could trust them with information and not experience their judgment. Beth discovered she could share her feelings and not be punished. And Brad learned that his parents had his best interest at heart.

The Thompsons' experience points to the fact that family support speeds the healing process for child victims of sexual assault. Children recover more quickly and experience fewer long-term effects when parents take an active role in their recovery.

Overcoming Adversity Through Resilience

We know that children can thrive in spite of their traumas. Many children who experienced adversity not only move beyond their sexual abuse but seem to become stronger individuals.

Researchers have identified a number of resilient characteristics, including responsiveness, flexibility, empathy and caring, communication skills, and a sense of humor.

Resiliency is the ability to face life with a will to win, see life's obstacles as challenges, and be able to bounce back from setbacks. In addition to the other characteristics, here are some more resilient qualities. You can help your child to become resilient by demonstrating these qualities yourself:

- Social competence—the ability to adapt to different social situations and seek out helpers or advocates.

Social adapters are able to ask for help and establish positive relationships.

- The ability to plan and problem-solve—knowing how to anticipate trouble or obstacles and make plans to circumvent them. Recognizing and steering clear of potentially physically dangerous situations is one example.

- Adaptive distancing—the ability to "love from afar." It is being aware of another's limitations but having the capacity to love her anyway without taking on excessive responsibility for her troubles or becoming enmeshed in her problems.

- Centeredness, or an inner locus of control—a sense of self and having a bottom line when it pertains to certain values. Centered people won't place values in jeopardy by crossing a self-determined line.

- Spirituality—having a strong belief in a higher being that guides us through life. Spiritual people report praying, seeking nature, or honoring a deceased relative when they discuss spirituality.

- High expectations and a sense of a future—a sense of optimism and tending to view the world from a "half full" perspective. You believe that things do get better and at some point you'll realize their goals.

- A significant caring adult—having an association with one caring adult even when the adult is not particularly close. This is the largest contributor in building resiliency in children. An accomplished man shared his story when he said, "My father was murdered when I was five years old, and my mom remarried a Klu Klux

Klan member. This wasn't a good thing because I'm a person of color. The only way to escape my family's absurd behavior was to visit the public library. I spent hours there and was introduced to the classics by the caring librarians, who seemed to understand the needs of a young boy. They made a significant difference in my life."

- Humor—the ability to laugh at cruelty and adjust your view on adversity. It provides a tool to relieve stress and engage adults. People who use humor are more likely to build relationships faster and receive positive feedback.

HEALTHY STEPS

The molestation was something the Thompsons will never forget. Scott will always remember that an older authority figure treated him as a sexual object. His folks couldn't remove that experience or substitute a different reality.

Scott came away from the experience understanding that he could live through a crisis and become a better person because of it. Sexual abuse was a terrible way to learn about compassion, but Scott became a more compassionate child because of his assault. His parents noticed his sensitivity when he volunteered to spend time with his grandmother in her new home and when he helped bathe animals at their local animal shelter.

Janet and Bill had never anticipated grieving a sexual assault experienced by one of their children. They had faced an extremely difficult experience, wishing throughout that one of them had been harmed rather than their son.

Scott's brother and sister wouldn't forget the strangers who came to their home the day after Janet made the report either. But they understood the unity and strength of being part of a family that banded together during a time of crisis.

One of the healthiest steps you can take is to recognize that it's unrealistic to believe your family will be the same after your child has disclosed her abuse. By virtue of the fact that your child has been violated, your family will be affected as well. No family remains the same after this experience.

It's important to remember you are not alone. Reach out to people who can advise and help you. Others have survived similar experiences to find their bearings again and give meaning to their suffering. You have the capacity to take a catastrophe and transform it into a positive life lesson. People who move beyond their tragedies also report that they have a renewed appreciation for life.

With your continued love and guidance, your child can have a good life. And with supportive therapy, your family can move beyond her sexual molestation and allow it to take its proper place in your past. The future does hold bright promises.

Glossary

This glossary is provided to familiarize you with words or phrases that appear in this book. Although the definitions of these words may differ by source, the definitions provided here are generally accepted.

ABUSER A person believed or known to have sexually molested a child. Used interchangeably with assailant, molester, perpetrator, and defendant.

ACT OUT To behave in an oppositional or defiant manner.

ACUTE STRESS Symptoms that reflect an anxious condition that lasts up to one month following a traumatic experience.

ADDRESS To acknowledge and propose a resolution.

ADMISSIBLE Acceptable as evidence in a court of law. What is admissible in one jurisdiction may not be admissible in another.

ADVOCACY Active support of a person, cause, idea, or policy.

ADVOCATE (noun) Someone who supports a person, cause, idea, or policy. (verb) To speak on behalf of or to help protect the rights of another person or cause.

AGE APPROPRIATE Psychological or physical functions that fall within what is considered normal for a given age range.

ALLEGATION An accusation made by a person or system against a person.

ALLEGE To insinuate or declare.

AMYGDALA An almond-shaped region in the brain that registers fear. One of its main jobs is to determine what's scary, although it also plays a role in registering reward.

ANATOMICALLY CORRECT A doll or drawing that depicts the human body faithfully. In the past, anatomically correct dolls have been used with children to demonstrate their sexual abuse. Anatomically correct drawings have been used more in recent years.

ARRAIGNMENT A court appearance by an accused person to hear the charges being made against him or her.

ASSAILANT The perpetrator of a sexual assault.

ASSAULT An unlawful attempt or threat to injure another person.

BARGAINING (As a grief stage) Engaging in diversions in an attempt to minimize or diminish the effects or consequences of child sexual abuse.

BELIEF SYSTEM A set of values or ideas tied to worldview and personal function.

CENTEREDNESS A quality relating to emotional balance and heightened personal awareness.

CHILD ABUSE ACCOMMODATION SYNDROME A classification of five of the most typical child sexual abuse victim reactions: secrecy; helplessness; entrapment and accommodation; delayed, conflicted, and unconvincing disclosure; and retention.

CHILD PROTECTION TEAM A child abuse crisis intervention agency that consults with law enforcement, child welfare, and medical professionals; not available in every community.

Also known as a *child advocacy team*, *advocacy center*, *sexual assault team*, or *children's crisis unit*.

COERCE To pressure another person verbally or physically to behave or think in a certain way.

CONTEST (verb) To legally dispute or disagree with an allegation or judgment and to seek to have it changed.

COPE To adjust behaviors and attitudes in order to reconcile or accommodate certain conditions.

COPING MECHANISMS Physical or emotional defenses that reflect attempts at suppressing feelings, emotions, or anxiety associated with a past traumatic experience.

CORTISOL A stress hormone that responds to danger signals and prepares the body for fight or flight. It regulates sleep-wake cycles, mental arousal, and the immune system. It can also affect the ability to speak.

CYBERSEX In this book, on-line engagement pertaining to sexual discussion or behaviors that can subsequently lead to personal contact and child sexual abuse.

DEFENDANT The person legally charged with committing an unlawful act.

DEMAND FOR DISCOVERY Defense request to examine all evidence against the defendant to be presented in court.

DENDRITES Fibers extending from the body of the neuron, which receive incoming signals from other neurons in the brain.

DEPENDENCY A legal condition established to protect a child's welfare, in which a child becomes temporarily a dependent of the state and subject to a state agency's supervision.

DEPOSITION A sworn statement.

DISCLOSURE A child's statement that sexual abuse has occurred.

DISSOCIATION A method of mentally escaping while the sexual abuse occurs. The brain accommodates a separation between the mind and the body. One example is "leaving the body and floating on the ceiling." Dissociation can occur later, when a child is triggered into a freezing or fight-or-flight response. This type of dissociation may be experienced as a numbing sensation or other mental separation from the actual events and could include spontaneous daydreaming.

DNA (DEOXYRIBONUCLEIC ACID) Nucleic acids in the nucleus of a cell; DNA, along with genes, creates the blueprint used to create and destroy life. DNA is usually collected by swabbing the mouth.

DOCKET The court schedule.

DYSFUNCTIONAL (Pertaining to family) The inability to coordinate family unity.

EEG Electroencephalographic photographs of localized brain activity.

ELICIT To obtain information.

ENVIRONMENT The personal circumstances and conditions that have an impact on a child.

EXAGGERATED STARTLE RESPONSE An abnormally exaggerated fear response triggered by a symbolic or literal association to the sexual abuse (for example, a car backfires and a child screams, or a back door opens and a child begins to panic).

EXTENDED FAMILY Family members other than primary caregivers and their children: aunts and uncles, cousins, and in-laws, for example.

EYE MOVEMENT DESENSITIZATION REPROCESSING (EMDR) A neural linguistic and memory accessing technique that assists with alleviating distress associated with traumatic memories.

FAMILIAL Pertaining to the family.

FELONY A crime determined as more serious than others (called *misdemeanors*). Examples are manslaughter, murder, and rape.

FUNCTIONAL MAGNETIC RESONANCE IMAGING (FMRI) A technique that provides a detailed view of brain structure.

GENITALIA The reproductive organs. In males, the penis, testicles, and prostate. In females, the vulva, vagina, uterus (womb), ovaries (egg area), and fallopian tubes (the path between the ovaries and uterus).

GENITALS External (outside the body) reproductive organs.

GRIEF A condition present as a result of experiencing loss or disappointment.

GUARDIAN AD LITEM A volunteer or professional person assigned by the court to protect and make recommendations that are in the interest of a child.

HEALING PROCESS The general recovery overview from disclosure to resolution of child sexual abuse.

HIDDEN AGENDA Unspoken intentions.

HIPPOCAMPUS A brain region that is associated with learning and memory. It is responsible for making associations and plays a role in conscious memory as well as consolidating memories.

HYMEN The membrane covering the entrance to the vagina. It can be torn during the first intercourse or insertion of an object into the vagina. This action describes the phrase "losing one's virginity."

HYPERAROUSAL Sensitivity to cues that represent possible danger triggering an automatic fear response.

INCEST Blood, social, or marital relationship between the sexual offender and the child sexual abuse victim.

INCESTUOUS Describes a type of sexual relationship. See *incest*.

INDICTMENT (Pronounced in-dight'-ment) A formal legal accusation that someone has committed a particular crime.

ISSUES Personal or systemic problematic conditions, such as a bad temper, personal conflict, poor coping skills, or family conflict.

JURISDICTION The range of territory over which laws, controls, and authority applies.

LASCIVIOUS Something that excites sexual desires. See *lewd*.

LEWD Commonly referred to as indecent.

LIMBIC SYSTEM Located in the lower midbrain, it connects to brain regions such as the hippocampus and the cerebral cortex, where abstract thinking occurs. The limbic system sorts through sensory input and identifies whether they are good, bad, or neutral. Emotions generated in this region help humans adapt to their environment.

MAGISTRATE A person with authority to administer and enforce laws.

MANDATE (noun) An enforceable command or instruction; usually issued by the court or an agency with legal authority.

MOLEST (noun) The name given to sexual assault.

MOLESTATION Involving, exposing, or even asking children to engage in any sexual activity or exhibition. This can include wrongful clothed or unclothed touching, exposure to pornographic materials, acts of bestiality, coercing sexual acts between children, cybersex, or performing indecent sexual acts in the presence of a child.

MOLESTER The person committing the act of molestation (used interchangeably with *abuser, perpetrator, defendant,* and *assailant*).

MORALITY External values superimposed on societies and individuals.

NEURON A nerve cell that underlies the basis for brain formation. Babies have over 1 billion at birth. These cells receive, analyze, coordinate, and transmit information.

NONOFFFENDING PARENT The parent or caregiver who did not knowingly participate in the sexual molestation of his or her child.

NORADRENALINE An alarm hormone that compels the brain to respond to danger, producing adrenaline and other chemicals that prepare the body for fight or flight. It is thought that noradrenaline imbalance may create impulsive or cold-blooded violence.

NORMS Standard behavior models or patterns.

PERPETRATOR Used here to indicate the person committing a molestation (used interchangeably with *abuser*, *molester*, *assailant*, and *defendant*).

PLAINTIFF The legal term for a person who has alleged harm.

POSITRON EMISSION TOMOGRAPHY (PET) Measures the activity of cells in different areas of the brain.

POSTTRAUMATIC STRESS Symptoms that reflect an anxious condition lasting beyond one month following a traumatic experience.

PREFERENTIAL CHILD MOLESTER A term used to describe a type of child sex offender who is compulsively sexually aroused by prepubescent children (a pedophile) or postpubescent males (a hebophile). The sexual arousal patterns are often fixed and can be difficult to treat.

PROSECUTING ATTORNEY The state's legal representative in cases determined as unlawful acts against society. Also known as the *district attorney*, *magistrate*, *county or city attorney*, or *state's attorney*.

REALITY CHECK A means of comparing personally perceived norms to established norms.

RESOLUTION Resolving or reconciling a problem.

SECONDARY TRAUMATIC STRESS Symptoms that reflect vicarious experience of a victim's distress. Also called *Compassion Fatigue*.

SIBLING Brother or sister.

SITUATIONAL CHILD MOLESTER A type of child sex offender who is not compulsively drawn to children but will engage them in sexual acts for a variety of reasons.

STATE'S ATTORNEY See *prosecuting attorney*.

SURVIVOR A child sexual assault victim.

THERAPIST A trained and licensed psychotherapy counselor.

THERAPY Receiving psychological intervention and support from a trained, licensed therapist.

TRAUMA Severe disruptive action that affects physical and psychological function. Child sexual abuse is one form of trauma.

TRIGGERS Literal or symbolic associations to a traumatic experience that initiate a freezing or fight-or-flight body response.

VAGINAL Pertaining to the vagina.

VALID True, sound, based on correct assumption.

VULVA The outer lip-like surface at the opening to the vagina.

WARRANT A written legal arrest order.

Additional Information

Neural researchers, legislators, social workers, and court officials, as well as the general public, have gained more knowledge about child sexual abuse in recent years. The information provided here, arranged by chapter, represents the culmination of some of their efforts on behalf of traumatized children. It includes child sexual abuse legislation, refinement of sexual predator definitions, and important neural research pertaining to child sexual abuse.

CHAPTER ONE

Types of Adult Sexual Crimes Against Children and Youth

• Unlawful sexual transaction with a minor. A perpetrator knowingly induces, assists, or causes a minor (states vary in their definition of a minor, but it is usually under ages sixteen to nineteen) to engage in sexual activity.

• Use of a minor in a sexual performance. Using a minor in a sexual performance such as a play, motion picture, photograph, or dance. *Performance* means any visual representation exhibited before one or more persons and includes sexual conduct. *Sexual conduct* is broadly defined and includes:

acts of masturbation, sexual intercourse—whether actual or simulated, physical contact with or willful intentional exhibition of the genitals, flagellation or excretion for the purpose of sexual stimulation or gratification or exposure in an obscene manner of clothed or unclothed human male or female genitals, pubic area or buttocks or the female breasts . . . in any motion picture, photograph or other visual representation including the Internet.

- Promoting a sexual performance by a minor.

A perpetrator promotes a sexual performance by a minor when knowing the character and content of what he produces, directs, or any performance that includes sexual conduct by a minor.

- Possession or distribution of matter portraying a sexual performance by a minor. A perpetrator knowingly has in his possession or control any matter that visually depicts an actual sexual performance by a minor child and if he (1) sends or causes to be sent this material, (2) sells or distributes the material, or (3) exhibits for profit or gain, distributes or possesses with intent to distribute any matter portraying the sexual performance of a minor.

- Promotes sale of or advertising material portraying a sexual performance of a minor.

A perpetrator knowingly, as a condition of the sale, allocation, consignment, or delivery for resale of any paper, magazine, book, publication, or other merchandise, requires that the purchaser or consignee receive any matter portraying a performance by a minor.

- Using minors to distribute material portraying a sexual performance of a minor.

Megan's Law

Megan Kanka was was raped and murdered in 1994 when she was seven years old. Her death triggered the federal Megan's Law, passed in 1996, which requires sex offender registration in all fifty states when sex offenders are released into the community and allows states to establish criteria about sex offender information that is made available to the public. Washington State's 1990 Community Protection Act included America's first law authorizing public notification when sex offenders are released back into the community.

Definitions of Exhibitionism, Pedophilia, and Voyeurism from the *Diagnostic and Statistical Manual of Mental Disorders*, Fourth Edition

Exhibitionism: "The exposure of one's genitals to a stranger."

Pedophilia: "A person that is involved in sexual activity with a prepubescent child (generally 13 years or younger). The individual with Pedophilia must be age 16 years or older and at least 5 years older than the child."

Voyeurism: "The act of observing unsuspecting individuals, usually strangers who are naked, in the act of disrobing or engaging in sexual activity."

Exhibitionists and voyeurs may engage in their behaviors with children, youth, or adults.

CHAPTER TWO

Amber Alert Act

Created in 1996 in some states but not passed nationally until April 2003, the National Amber Alert Act created a national communication network to establish broad-based Amber media alert systems in areas where none exists, establish standards for coordination, and provide funds for education and training from the U.S. Departments of Justice and Transportation. The act was named for Amber Hagerman, who was kidnapped and killed in Texas in the 1990s when she was nine years old.

CHAPTER THREE

False Memory Research

Researchers are discovering that the brain can be susceptible to sug-gestion. Experiments conducted at Western Washington Univer-sity demonstrated that a significant minority of participants could successfully be implanted with false memories. These people scored higher on scales that measure vividness of visual imagery than other participants who were not led by researchers. (Assigning a memory to the wrong sources, such as mistaking fantasy for reality or misin-terpreting the past, is called *misattribution*.)

Split brain research indicates that the left side of the brain can generate false reports. The left brain excels at developing schemata, or a general perceptual outline, and has an ability to determine the source of a memory based on the surrounding events. The right brain is good at perceiving stimulus. The left brain looks for order and reason when there is none, and so it continues to make mis-takes that include constructing a "potential past" as opposed to a true one.

Elizabeth Loftus, Ph.D., at the University of California believes that some people may be more suggestible than others and could even be convinced they are responsible for crimes they did not com-mit. Richard McNally, Ph.D., from Harvard University, studied false memory subjects; as they told their fabricated stories, their bodies responded by perspiring and developing higher heart rates.

CHAPTER FOUR

Sexual Abuse and Normal Brain Function

- When children are not exposed to supportive environ-ments, neural chemical imbalances may emerge that can change their ability to control themselves and bond with others.

- Chronic stress can cause the neurons in the hippocampus, the brain's memory center, to lose dendrites and spines due to ongoing cortisol released when someone is frightened. Consequently, the hippocampus can shrink in size, limiting this area's memory sorting and organizing function. Positron emission topography scans substantiate abnormal brain function.

- Chronic activation of neuronal pathways (highways) involved in the fear response can wear out certain brain areas and create permanent "memories" that shape a child's perception or response to the environment even after her circumstances improve. Efforts to suppress her intrusive thoughts can raise her anxiety, and a vicious cycle that involves triggers, invasive thoughts, and attempts to control her physical and emotional responses can occur.

- Many sexually abused children and youth experience mood disorder because trauma can affect the development of their subcortical and limbic systems. Irritability in the limbic system can cause panic.

- Chronic fear can cause damage to the amygdala, the brain region that regulates fear. Over time, an automatic fear response called *hyperarousal* may occur.

- Bruce Perry, M.D., has stated that it's not unusual for intelligent children to have learning problems and to be diagnosed with disabilities when they have experienced disturbing events.

Directed Forgetting

Youth who remember their abuse after years of no recollection can experience something called *directed forgetting*. During or after their sexual assault, children are directed, or given suggestions, to forget their abuse. As a result, they consciously avoid those memories, repeatedly inhibiting access to them. But strong cues or triggers can elicit emotions felt at the time of abuse, and a memory will then surface. Psychologist Jonathan Schooler documented a case involving a thirty-year-old man who suddenly remembered being sexually molested at age twelve by a parish priest. Prior to watching a movie, which served as the trigger, the man had had no memory of being abused.

Relationship of Trauma to Violence and Aggression in Children

Children who have experienced chronic and ongoing abuse or neglect can later become persistently hyperaroused and vigilant about their personal safety. Biologist Dr. Saul Schanberg has said, "A stressful environment can cause genes important for survival to become overly expressed, making human beings more aggressive and violent."

Resources

CHAPTER ONE

American Psychiatric Association. *Diagnostic and Statistical Manual of Mental Disorders*. (4th ed.) Washington, D.C.: American Psychiatric Association, 1994.

Brohl, K. *The New Miracle Workers: Overcoming Contemporary Challenges in Child Welfare Work*. Washington, D.C.: Child Welfare League of America, 2003.

"Child Abuse and Neglect." [webmd.aol.com/content/healthwise/135/33513.htm]. Mar. 11, 2003.

Child Welfare League of America. "Child Abuse and Neglect." Washington, D.C.: Child Welfare League of America, 2000.

Family Violence Task Force. Office of the Attorney General. [www.attorneygeneral.gov/family/misc/stats.cfm]. Mar. 12, 2003.

Gunder, R. "The Sexual Attitudes of Mental Health Professionals Providing Clinical Services to Sexual Offenders." Unpublished doctoral dissertation, Institute for Advanced Study of Human Sexuality, 1997.

Jones, R. L., and Kaufman, L. "Ten-Year-Old Murder Suspect Had Worried His Neighbors." *New York Times*, Mar. 29, 2003.

KlassKids Foundation. "Megan's Law by State." [KlassKids.org]. 2002.

Lanning, K. V. *Child Molesters: A Behavioral Analysis*. Alexandria, Va.: National Center for Missing and Exploited Children, 1992.

Levy, T. M., and Orlans, M. *Attachment, Trauma and Healing*. Washington, D.C.: CWLA Press, 1998.

"National Child Abuse and Neglect Statistical Fact Sheet." [www.whme.af.mil/
    Teamhelp/FAST_FACTS/NATIONAL_CHILD_ABUSE_ANS. . .].
    Jan. 24, 2003.
Treen, D. "Parents Question School's Security." (Jacksonville) *Florida Times
    Union*, Apr. 2, 2003.

CHAPTER TWO

Boyle, P. "Amber Alert Held Hostage by Politics." *Youth Today*, 2003, *12*(4), 15.
Brohl, K., and Potter, J. *When Your Child Has Been Molested.* (1st ed.) San
    Francisco: New Lexington Press, 1988.
Child Welfare League of America. "Fact Sheet." Washington, D.C.: Child
    Welfare League of America, 2000.
Fairfax County Family Services. "Child Sexual Abuse Fact Sheet." Fairfax, Va.:
    Fairfax County Family Services, July 2000.

CHAPTER THREE

Blom, E. "Danger Online: Child Abusers Exploit New Opportunities Via
    Internet." (Portland) *Maine Telegram*, Oct. 11, 1998, p. 1A.
Brusca, C. T. "What Is the Stockholm Syndrome?" *Peace Encyclopedia.*
    [www.yahoodi.com/peace/stockholm.html]. 1998.
"False Memories Easy to Induce, Study Shows." (Jacksonville) *Florida Times
    Union*, Feb. 24, 2003.
Fine, L. "Paying Attention." *Education Week*, May 2001.
"Gloomy Gus Might Blame Brain." (Jacksonville) *Florida Times Union*, Feb. 17,
    2002.
"School Girl 13, Found Slain; Chat Room Partner a Suspect." (Jacksonville)
    Florida Times Union, May 22, 2002.
Slavin, P. "How Safe Are Children on the Internet?" *Children's Voice*, 2002,
    11(1), 24–28.
"Studies Link Child Abuse to Brain Changes." *Children's Voice*, 2002, *11*(3).

CHAPTER FOUR

Brohl, K. *Working with Traumatized Children: A Handbook for Healing.* Washing-
    ton, D.C.: CWLA Press, 1996.

California Office of Criminal Justice Planning. "Tips to Parents." Sacramento: Child Sexual Abuse Prevention, Office of Criminal Justice Planning, State of California, 2002.

Cowley, G. "Our Bodies, Our Fears," *Newsweek*, Feb. 24, 2003.

Damasio, A. R. "How the Brain Creates the Mind." *Scientific American*, Aug. 31, 2002.

Davidson, J.R.T. "Repairing the Shattered Self: Recovering from Trauma." *Clinical Psychiatry*, 1997 (special issue), pp. 4–9.

Gunnar, M. R. *Early Adversity and the Development of Stress Reactivity and Regulations*. Bethesda, Md.: National Institutes of Health, 2000.

Johnson, D., and Christenson, E. "Finding Elizabeth." *Newsweek*, Mar. 24, 2003.

Kotulak, R. *Inside the Brain: Revolutionary Discoveries of How the Mind Works*. Kansas City, Mo.: Andrews McMeel Publishing, 1996.

National Center for Injury Prevention and Control. "Suicide Prevention Fact Sheet." Washington, D.C.: National Center for Injury Prevention and Control, 1998.

National Institutes of Health. "Learning Disabilities." Decade of the Brain, Bethesda, Md.: National Institutes of Health, 2002.

Perry, B. D. *Neurodevelopment and the Psychophysiology of Trauma 1: Conceptual Considerations for Clinical Work with Maltreated Children*. Houston: Baylor College of Medicine, 1992.

Perry, B. D. *Traumatized Children: How Childhood Trauma Influences Brain Development*. Houston: Baylor College of Medicine, 1998.

Schacter, D. L. *The Seven Sins of Memory: How the Mind Forgets and Remembers*. Boston: Houghton Mifflin, 2002.

Van der Kolk, B. A., and McFarlane, A. C. *Traumatic Stress*. New York: Guilford Press, 1996.

Weinstein, J., and Weinstein, R. "Neuropsychological Consequences of Child Neglect and Their Implication for Social Policy." [www.calib.com/nccanch/cbconference/resourcebook/72.cfm]. 2000.

Wolfe, P., and Brandt, R. "What Do We Know from Brain Research?" *Educational Leadership*, 1998, 56(3), 8–13.

CHAPTER SIX

Children's Crisis Center. "CMS Child Protection Team Telemedicine Network." Jacksonville, Fla.: Children's Crisis Center, 2003.

CHAPTER EIGHT

Brohl, K., and Potter, J. C. *When Your Child Has Been Molested: A Parents' Guide to Healing and Recovery.* (1st ed.) San Francisco: New Lexington Press, 1988.

Figley, C. R. (ed.). *Compassion Fatigue: Coping with Secondary Traumatic Stress Disorder in Those Who Treat the Traumatized.* New York: Brunner/Mazel, 1995.

CHAPTER NINE

Brohl, K., and Potter, J. C. *When Your Child Has Been Molested: A Parents' Guide to Healing and Recovery.* (1st ed.) San Francisco: New Lexington Press, 1988.

"What Is the Theoretical Basis for EMDR?" [www.emdr.com/ql.htm]. Mar. 2003.

CHAPTER TEN

Barker, P. *Using Metaphors in Psychotherapy.* New York: Brunner/Mazel, 1985.

Brohl, K. *Working with Traumatized Children: A Handbook for Healing.* Washington, D.C.: Child Welfare League of America, 1996.

Ertes, C. P. *Women Who Run with the Wolves: Myths and Stories of the Wild Woman Archetypes.* New York: Ballantine, 1992.

Mattson, M. "Helping Children to Control Chronic Emotional Eruptions." (Jacksonville) *Florida Times Union*, Apr. 8, 2003, pp. C1, C2.

Rosen, E. *My Voice Will Go with You: The Teaching Tales of Milton H. Erickson MD.* New York: Norton, 1982.

About the Authors

Kathryn Brohl, M.A., a licensed marriage and family therapist, has worked in child welfare for over thirty years. She is the author of three additional books and coeditor of another. She has written and produced child welfare advocacy training videos and continues training and consulting with child welfare advocates on trauma issues throughout the United States, Canada, and Australia. She has also cohosted a nationally syndicated radio program. Kathryn lives in Florida with her husband.

Joyce Case Potter recently opted to focus her professional energies entirely on writing for children after twenty years as a full-time freelance writer. She lives in Winston-Salem, North Carolina, with her husband, Tony, and enjoys being an active member in the Society of Children's Book Writers and Illustrators' Carolinas region.

Index

A

Abrams, P. (Thompson family therapist), 59, 60, 69, 78, 79, 82, 100, 104, 131–134, 139, 140, 162, 163, 180

Abuse. *See* Child sexual abuse; Physical abuse

Acceptance grief stage, 95–97; behaviors and attitudes, 97–98

Acquaintance rape, 9–10, 32

Advocacy, 189; victim, 63

Age, 8

Alcohol, 5, 7, 8, 40, 55

Altered Personality Disorder, 41

Amygdala, 190, 201

Andrews, P., 60–62

Anger, 42, 43, 89–90; inappropriate ways to express, 90–91; managing child's, 119–121

Animals, aggression toward, 53

Ann's story, 34–35

Antisocial behavior, 53

Anxiety, 29, 43, 53, 74, 75, 83–85

Appearances, 160–161

Appetite, disturbance in, 54

Arousal, 46

Arraignment, 24, 190

Assault, sexual, 190; and kidnapping, 39–40; and rape, 39–40; by strangers, 38; via Internet, 38–39

Attachment disorders, 8

B

Bargaining stage, 94–95, 190

Behavior: aggressive, 53; antisocial, 53; changes in, 54; impulsive, 7; mimicry of adult sexual, 56; regressive, 54

Bipolar disorder, 111

Blame, 33, 34

Breathing, 83–84

Bruce, P., 201

Bullies, 9–10

C

Caregiver abandonment, fear of, 13–14

Case coordinators, 63

CCRC. *See* Crimes Against Children Research Center (CCRC; University of New Hampshire)

Cell phones, 12

Centeredness, 190

Check-in calls, 80

Child Abuse Accommodation Syndrome, 168, 190

Child abuse examiner, 60

Child, abused: believing, 31–33; blaming, in incest, 168–169; importance of listening to, 43–44; removal of, from home, 168; and sexual abuse reports, 33–35; support of, after disclosure, 27–44; unsupported, 40–43

Child Accommodation Syndrome, 35
Child advocacy center, 20
Child molesters: and bullies, 9–10; facts about, 4–6; preferential, 6–8; situational, 6–8; types of, 6–8
Child Protection Team, 18–19, 59–62, 69, 77, 104, 190, 191
Child sexual abuse: definition of, 3–4; disclosure of, 1–3; investigation and prosecution of, 19–25; learning about, 11–15; and normal brain function, 200–204; reporting, 17–19; signs of, 45–58; statistics, 13
Child Welfare League of America Website, 62
Children molesters, 6, 8–11; and bullies, 9–10; and family members, 9; and institutional settings, 10; intervention for, 6; and siblings, 9
Children's Crisis Unit, 61
Children's Defense Fund Website, 62
Club drugs, 9–10
Community pressure, 18
Community Protection Act (Washington State, 1990), 199
Compassion fatigue, 98–99. See also Secondary traumatic stress (STS)
Compulsive sexualization, 8
Concentration, 54
Conduct disorders, 8
Confidence, 40
Confidentiality, child's, 108
Continuances, 25, 81–82
Coping skills, 7, 191
Cortisol, 191, 201
Counseling: benefit of, for family members, 132–134; and counseling professionals, 19; and handling frustration, 78–79; realistic expectations about, 112–114
Counselors: considerations about, 110–111; selection of, 103–104; and therapist selection questions, 105–110; working with, 103–104. See also Therapists

County Sheriff's Department, 59, 60
Court: civil, 26; criminal, 25; family, 26; juvenile, 25; probate, 25; types of, 25–26
Court appearance: and appearance of self as witness, 160–161; and depositions, 154–155; outcome of, for Thompson's, 161–162; preparation of child for, 156–160; preparing for, 154–155; and videotaped testimony, 155; and when verdict is "not guilty," 161–162
Crimes Against Children Research Center (CCRC; University of New Hampshire), 38–39
Criminal charges, 22
Culture, 18
Custody, 176

D
DaCosta's syndrome, 51
Defense attorney: at deposition, 154–155; role of, in judicial process, 81–82
Delay, 80, 81. See also Continuances
Demand for discovery, 24, 191
Dendrites, 191, 201
Denial grief stage, 87–89
Department of Children and Families, 59, 60
Depositions, 154–155, 191
Depression, 42–43, 53, 91–94; grief and, 91–94; symptoms, 93–94
Detachment, 83
Devlin, J. (child abuse examiner for Thompson family), 60–62
Diagnostic and Statistical Manual of Mental Health Disorders (American Psychiatric Association), 11, 199
Directed forgetting, 201–202
Disclosure, 1–3, 191; first response to, 27–30; support after, 27–44
Disease, as cause of sexual abuse, 4–5
Dissociation, 41, 42, 192
Distorted thinking, 41, 42

DNA (Deoxyribonucleic Acid), 11, 72, 192
Docket, 23, 192; sounding, 25
Drug use, 5, 7, 8, 40, 58

E

Eastwood, C., 137
Eating disorders, 43
Examination, 21
Exhibitionism, 11, 199
Experimentation, 47
Extended family, 192; answering comments of, 150–151; dealing with, 145–152; helping child when questioned by, 151–152; possible remarks of, 149–150; and respecting child's feelings, 147–148; responding to comments and actions of, 148–149; and special considerations with regard to incest, 150; what to keep in mind when talking to, 146–147
Eye Movement Desensitization Reprocessing (EMDR), 106, 111, 192

F

False memory research, 200
Family communication: breakdown signs, 135–136; and challenging old communication habits, 136–137; and secrecy, 138–139; strengthening, 135–144; and therapy, 144; and Thompson experience, 137–142; tips for improving, 142–144
Family members, 20; and counseling, 132–134; and dealing with feelings, 131–132; impact of child abuse on, 129–134
Family recovery, 179–183; factors that contribute to, 183–184; and healthy steps, 186–187; and resilience, 184–186
Fears: irrational, 53; overcoming, 19–25
Feelings: dealing with own, 131–132

Fight-or-flight response, 49
Finkelhor, D., 39
Flashbacks, 52
Forensic interview. See Formal interview
Forgiveness, 174
Formal interview, 21, 65–75; and adolescent youth, 71–72; after, 72–74; and establishing reasonable expectations with child, 67–68; and forensic physical examination, 70–72; preparation for, 67; and prepubescent children, 71
Freezing response, 5, 49
Frustration, and counseling, 78–79

G

GHB, 9–10
Good touch, 169
Grampa Thompson's Scary Journey, 122–124
Grief, 193; acceptance stage of, 95–97; anger stage of, 89–90; bargaining stage of, 94–95; and behaviors to avoid, 89; guilt and depression stage of, 91–94; numbing and denial stage of, 87–89; response, 17; working through stages of, 98
Guardian ad litem, 154–155, 193
Guilt, 12, 14, 15, 91–94; and grief, 91–94

H

Hagerman, A. (Amber), 199
Harvard University, 200
Healthy steps, 186–187
Hebophiles, 6
Hedges, F. (child protection services investigator), 59–61, 69
Help, outside, 18
Hippocampus, 193, 201
HIV, 72
Hot line, abuse, 19
Hunter, B. (prosecuting attorney in Thompson case), 60, 61

Hyperarousal, 193, 201
Hypersensitivity, 53

I

Imagination, 32
Immigrant societies, 18
Incest, 13, 193; additional pressures from, 170–171; and custody or visitation allegations, 176; dealing with, 177; definition of, 165–166; examples of, 165–166; and relative who has molested before, 166; and removal of child from home, 168; response to, 167–168; and sex offender programs, 175–176; taking responsibility in, 173–174; when child becomes pregnant from, 171–173; when parents blame child in, 168–169; when sexual abuse is, 165–177; when there is denial to forgive child's sexual assailant, 174
Indicators, 12
Insanity, 5
Institutional settings, 10
Insular societies, 18
Intercourse, sexual, 4, 37; simulated, 37
Internet, 12, 38–39: national child welfare associations on, 62
Intervention, medication, 109
Interventions, 11
Intimacy, 36
Investigation, 19–25

J

Jack's story, 50
Johnson, S. (case coordinator for Thompsons), 59, 61, 69, 77
Johnson, V., 46
Judge, 23
Judgment, 28
Judicial process: confusions about, 79–81; counseling for frustration due to, 78–79; defense attorney's role in, 81–82; and detachment, 83; and how cases are handled, 79;

length of time for, 77–78; and when case does not go to trial, 81

K

Kanka, M., 198–199
Kidnapping, 2, 39–40

L

Labels, 14
Law enforcement, 20
Lawyer, court-appointed, 24
Lie detector, 22
Limbic system, 194, 201
Loftus, E., 200
Lying, 32, 33

M

Magical thinking, 42
Magistrate, 23
Males, 13
Mania, 53
Maria's story, 28
Markers, abuse, 12, 14
Masters, W. H., 46
Masturbation, 54; mutual, 47
McNally, R., 200
Medication intervention, 109
Megan's Law, 11, 198–199
Megan's story, 149–150
Memory: false, 30; problems, 54
Menstruation, 47
Metaphor, 121
Misattribution, 200
Modesty, 47
Mood disorders, 42, 53, 201
Mr. Rogers' Neighborhood (television program), 84

N

National Amber Alert Act, 199
National Center for Missing and Exploited Children Website, 62
National Institute of Mental Health, 57
Native American tribal protocol, 18
Neural biology technique, 106, 111

Neurochemical imbalance, 42–43, 49–50, 200, 201
Neuronal pathways, 195, 201
Nightmares, 53
Nocturnal emissions, 47
Numbing grief stage, 87–89

O

Others: answering comments of, 150–151; helping child when questioned by, 151–152; possible remarks of, 149–150; and respecting child's feelings, 147–148; responding to comments and reactions of, 148–149; what to keep in mind when talking to, 146–147

P

Pam and Monique's story, 169–170
Parents: reactions of, 13; responses of, at formal interview, 74
Pedophilia, 6, 7, 11, 199
Penetration, 37
Performance, sexual, 197–198
Phone sex, 39
Physical abuse, 7
Physical contact, 3–4
Physical examination, forensic, 70–72; results of, 72
Placement, 22
Pornography, 36, 39, 197–198
Positron emission topography, 201
Posttraumatic Stress Syndrome/ Disorder, 43, 51; acute stress and, 48–49; physical condition behind, 49–52
Potential past, 200
Preferential child molesters, 6–8, 109, 195
Prefiling agreement, 23–24
Pregnancy, 54
Prejudices, 176
Prevention advocates, 63
Probable cause, 23
Professional support team, 59–63
Professionals, 18–19

Profiles, 31
Prosecuting attorney, 19–25, 60, 61, 79, 154–155, 195
Psychological distance, 80
Psychological testing, 110
PTSD. See Posttraumatic Stress Syndrome/Disorder
Public defender, 24
Punishment, 31

R

Rage, 43
Rape, 39–40, 48
Rapid response advocacy, 63
Rationalization, 8, 23
Recanting, 35
Recovery, child's: feeling safe and having positive self-perception in, 115–127; helping toward, 115–127; and managing child's anger, 119–121; recognition of, 179–187; role of storytelling in, 121–127
Recreational activities, 84
Reenactment signs, 56
Registration, sex offender, 11
Rejection, 34
Relationships, 8, 42
Religious sects, 18
Remorse, 7
Resilience, 184–186
Response: to child, 30–31; first, after disclosure, 27–30; negative, 28
Responsibility, in incest, 173–174
Ritual, 37
Rogers, F., 84
Routines, 29; compulsive, 54

S

Safe environment, 21
Safe person, 12
Safety plan, building, 182–183
Safety precautions, extreme, 54
Schanberg, S., 202
Schizophrenia, 111
Schooler, J., 202
Schwarzenegger, A., 137

Secondary traumatic stress (STS), 196; and compassion fatigue, 98–99; working through, 99–100

Seduction: by children, 4, 35, 55; progress of, 36–37

Self-control, 7

Self-involvement, 13–14

Self-mutilation, 54

Sentencing guidelines, 80

Serenity prayer, 96

Sex offenders: facts about, 4–6; identity of, 4; prosecution of, 79; treatment program, 23, 175–176; types of, 6–8, 109

Sexual abuse unit (Department of Children and Families), 59

Sexual arousal, negative, 43

Sexual Assault Team, Advocacy Center, 61

Sexual conduct, types of, 197–198

Sexual crimes, types of, against children, 197–198

Sexual Crimes Unit (County Sheriff's Department), 59, 60

Sexual development, 45–48

Sexual intimacy, 8

Sexualization, compulsive, 8

Sexually transmitted disease (STD), 71, 72

Shame, 14, 23

Shawn's story, 172–173

Siblings, and sexual indoctrination, 9

Signs: balance in reacting to, 56–58; reenactment, 54; sexual abuse, 53–55; suicide warning, 57

Situational child molesters, 6–8, 109, 196

Social skills, 8

Social workers, rapid-response, 63

Stockholm syndrome, 39, 40

Storytelling: example of, 122–124; power of, 127; and pulling story together, 124–126; role of, in recovery, 121–124; and sharing story, 126–127

Strangers, 37; assault by, 38–39

Stress, 7; acute, 48–52, 189; busting, 83–85; chronic, 201. See also Post-traumatic Stress Syndrome/Disorder

STS. See Secondary traumatic stress (STS)

Substance abuse, 5, 7, 8, 40, 58

Suicide, 57

Suspected abuse, 19

Symbols, 121, 125, 127

Symptoms, of sexual abuse, 53–55

T

Teenagers: as victims, 5

Telemedicine, 73

Texas, 199

Therapists: licensed clinical social workers (LCSWs), 104; licensed marriage and family (LMFTs), 104; and licensed mental health counselors (LMHCs), 105; and licensed psychologists (Ph.D.s or Psy.D.s), 105; and psychiatrists (M.D.s), 105; selection questions for, 105–110; types of, 104–105; working effectively with, 111–112. See also Counselors

Threats, 29

Translators, victim advocate, 63

Trauma, 33, 49, 51, 196; relationship of, to violence and aggression in children, 202

Triggers, 14, 51, 52–56; examples of, 52–53

Trust, 36, 41

U

United States Department of Justice, 199

United States Department of Transportation, 199

University of California, 200

University of New Hampshire, 38–39

V

Verdict, 160–161

Victim advocacy, 63

Videotape, 21, 155; and videotaping
    protocol, 108–109
Vietnamese culture, 18
Visitation, 176
Voyeurism, 199

W

Webster, Mr. (perpetrator in Thompson
    case), 2, 60, 133, 134, 141, 162, 163

*Webster's New World College Dictio-
    nary,* 14
Western Washington University,
    200
Witness, appearing as, 160–161
Women: with drug or alcohol addic-
    tions, 40; and sexual assault, 6,
    37
Wrong touch, 12, 32

CPSIA information can be obtained at www.ICGtesting.com
Printed in the USA
BVOW02n0921120714

358796BV00004B/7/P